LOVES ME...NOT

L❀VES ME... NOT

HOW TO SURVIVE (AND THRIVE!) IN THE FACE OF UNREQUITED LOVE

Samara O'Shea

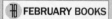 FEBRUARY BOOKS

Library of Congress Control Number: 2013942657
Loves Me . . . Not
How to Survive (and Thrive!) in the Face of Unrequited Love
Samara O'Shea
p.cm.
1. Self-Help / Personal Growth 2. Love & Romance
3. Happiness
Samara O'Shea—1st Edition

ISBN-13: 978-0-9849543-8-4
ISBN-10: 0-9849543-8-4

Cover Design by Veronica Zhu • Book Design by Casey Hampton

February Books
215 Park Avenue South
New York, NY 10003
www.februarybooks.com

Printed in the United States of America

This book is dedicated to two women named Winifred:

Winifred Harkins Stroup, my great-grandmother
A little love goes a long way. Yours has spread far and wide.
Your family is a lively, compassionate bunch.
I hope you're as proud of us as we are of you.

And her namesake:
Aunt Wynn
Aunt. Mother. Mentor. Friend. Role model.
A woman ahead of her time for as long as I can remember.

CONTENTS

I WANT YOU TO WANT ME

Nothing takes the taste out of peanut butter quite like unrequited love.

—Charlie Brown

Do you remember your first crush? Me too. I was in second grade and Joey Harshall sure did put an extra skip in my prepubescent step. First crushes are easy to recall because they mark the moment in our emotional evolution when we become significantly more aware of ourselves as individuals. We have a vibrant interest in something that exists outside our home, and it has nothing to do with our family. We can't even ask our parents if they'll buy it for us; it's a different kind of want altogether.

What follows the new awareness of a crush, almost immediately, is the fear that he—in this case, Joey—might not have a crush on *me*. This is why it's essential in elementary school to keep your feelings a secret and pretend as though you hate the boy while chasing him around with a purple baton. Even at a young age, we have a sense of what rejection is and know instinctively that it is not good.

I've had countless crushes since second grade, and I still consider the experience to be among life's best natural highs. You're excited for no reason. You carry around a sweet secret, and it makes you smile while standing in strange places—like the feminine hygiene aisle at CVS. You are one with nature, hence the stars in your eyes and butterflies in your stomach. Colors are brighter. Food tastes better. The sun feels warmer. And, somehow, every crush feels like the first crush. Each time, it's as if you've just been introduced to a part of yourself you didn't know existed.

As wonderful as crushes are, however, their lifespan is short; they tend to morph into a different form very quickly. Sometimes they evaporate completely and the source of the crush no longer elicits any reaction from you. In a more dangerous transmogrification, the crush boils over—it grows in intensity without reciprocation and becomes an obsession. Sometimes a crush solidifies into a relationship, in which case it usually upgrades to infatuation for a year or two and eventually becomes something less intense and more concrete. Unless, that is, the relationship ends against the will of one half of the (now ex-) couple. In that case, a wide-open wound remains that runs the risk of becoming an obsession if it doesn't heal properly.

Since many of us are at risk for catching an all-consuming obsession, if we don't have one already, and since obsession itself is on the rise (more on this in a moment) that's what we're going to focus on. Our purpose here is to stop unrequited love in its tracks so you can avoid reaching the point of obsession, walk triumphantly away from your unreturned feelings, and continue on the meaningful search for reciprocated feelings.

Unrequited love is tricky in that it's easy to slip into without noticing. As mentioned, it can start with a whimsical crush and—for some of us—become something that is seemingly selfless. You may find yourself willing to do *anything* for your stud muffin. You're primed to wash and wax his car, update his blog, and hem his pants. You feel gallant since you're willing to go so far out of your way for another person. It feels as if you're working toward something, and working hard is good, right?

In literature, people often die in the name of unrequited love. Classic examples include: Éponine in *Les Miserable*, Quasimodo in *The Hunchback of Notre Dame*, the mermaid in Hans Christian Andersen's original *The Little Mermaid* (yes it's true, and I'll tell the *real* story in a bit). Cyrano in *Cyrano de Bergerac* didn't die right away, but he lived a sullen, unfulfilled life because of unrequited love. Why do authors gravitate toward this scenario? Well, it does make for a good story. But losing your life, either literally or figuratively, in the name of someone who won't give you the time of day is not valiant, and it doesn't translate well into reality. I know because I've wasted countless hours of my life scheming, plotting, and praying for some guy to give me the attention I was willing to give him. I'd adamantly protest to my friends, "How can you ask me to give up on this? Isn't love worth fighting for?" Love is worth fighting for, but what I was feeling wasn't love; it was neediness and obsession. You could *not* have convinced me of that at the time, however, and if you're in the throes of obsession, I don't expect to convince you either—not on this page anyway. I do hope you'll start agreeing with me around Chapter Six.

I mentioned that obsession is on the rise, and the reason probably won't surprise you. An article entitled "The Thoroughly Modern Guide to Breakups," in the February 2011 issue of *Psychology Today*, cites that due to our cyber-socializing, "hypersensitivity to rejection is on the rise and it's contributing to large increases in stalking behavior." Because Google and Facebook give us such an intimate look into other people's lives, it is increasingly difficult to know where to draw the line. Even if you aren't following your would-be heartthrob home, looking at his profile page every day is feeding your feelings in a negative way.

In junior high, romantic rejection is pretty straightforward; if a guy doesn't like you, he ignores you, makes fun of you, or calls you "kid." As an adult, though, it gets more complicated. A man might flirt openly with you at the water cooler but never ask you out. He might wine you, dine you, and take you to a bed and breakfast for the weekend—but that doesn't mean he wants to be exclusive. He might tell you he wants to be with you one day and then stop calling the next. A man might even ask you to marry him but then change his mind and send you an e-mail asking for the ring back (true story). All of these scenarios happen, and they have always happened. Long before e-mail was invented, people were breaking hearts in careless ways.

What hasn't always happened is the psychological study of love. That pursuit is roughly sixty years old, which is young in the research world. I've read a great deal on the subject and learned some important things. The most valuable lesson I've acquired is that (spoiler alert) unrequited love is not love at all, but, rather, it is a lack of love—for yourself. True love begins with a deep, authentic, steadfast, profound, and passionate love for yourself. It sounds unbearably narcissistic, I know, but I assure you it's not, and there is plenty of evidence coming your way. Without that love for yourself, you desperately search for someone (anyone!) to validate you, to complete you, and to be the cherry on top of the double-fudge sundae that is your life.

In fairness to us all, we as a society are taught to think that the answer to love's questions lie in another person. We are presented with images of perfect love from a young age. These images are usually comprised of a man, a woman, an evil queen, a glass slipper, talking animals, and a little fairy dust. The first problem with this ideal is that another person can't complete you. Complement you, yes; complete you, no.

We might be more informed if Erich Fromm had decided to become a cartoon animator instead of a psychoanalyst. In his book *The Art of Loving*, Fromm declares: "The first step to take is to become aware that love is an art, just as living is an art; if we want to learn how to love we must proceed in the same way we have to proceed if we want to learn any other art, say music, painting, carpentry, or the art of medicine or engineering." This goes against the common assumption that love is magical and mindless, that once you find the right person everything falls into place. Such assumptions do more harm than good, though; it can be disappointing when you realize that relationships take more work than you've been led to believe.

Learning love—how to develop it and retain it in a healthy way—involves study and practice, which begs the questions:

How the heck do you study love? And how do you practice it? I'm going to tell you. I'm still learning myself, but I will refer to sages who've been studying it for a long time. Also know that it took an excessive number of unreturned phone calls; being stood up multiple times; running into men I was dating while they're on dates; and full-force, self-demeaning behavior for me to learn any of this. These stories of mine, however, are about to come in handy as I tell them through the discerning eyes of retrospect. If I'm advising you not to do something, it means I've done it—probably more than twice.

A few notes: I am a heterosexual woman writing about my involvement (or lack thereof) with men, and for the sake of consistency I will refer to men and use the pronoun *he*. I want to give a shout-out to my homosexual sisters who I love dearly, and who have certainly had their hearts stomped all over. We women can be wicked. If you prefer to see a "she" where there's a "he," please do so. I also want to acknowledge the boys, homo- and heterosexual alike, who I also love truly, madly, and deeply. Men absolutely experience unrequited love—throughout history and well into today. It's unhealthy when a member of either sex is pursing someone relentlessly with little-to-no response from the other person. Included here are several stories of male heartache as experienced by my guy friends and a historical figure or two. However, statistically, men don't read books—especially relationship books—as often as women do, which is why the advice here is addressed exclusively to women. Names have been changed throughout the book for the most part—unless permission has been granted to use a real name. As for pseudonyms, I like to borrow them from pop culture characters.

To make sure we're on the same page, let's define unrequited love. For the purposes of this book, it is this: an unreciprocated longing for love that reveals itself in many ways. You
can admire a man from a distance and never tell him you have
romantic feelings for him. You can pursue a man tirelessly and
refuse to take no for an answer. You can date a man who doesn't
come right out and say no, he doesn't want a relationship with
you—most likely because he wants to keep sleeping with
you—but makes no promises either. You can be in a one-sided
relationship, meaning you both say you're committed but all of
the compromises are made by you and few by him. You can be
in long-term partnership with reciprocal love, when (in one of
life's more unfair circumstances) your beloved leaves unexpectedly one day and you're left to recover.

The advice in this book speaks largely to those admiring or
obsessing from a distance; those getting the runaround from a
guy in the first few months of dating; those who stop hearing
from a guy after several dates; or those sleeping with ambigu-
ously intentioned boys. The personal stories herein, however,
address a wide variety of circumstances. They include the
aforementioned dating scenarios; marriages that end after two
years or twenty years; unrequited affairs; and a lovelorn, sev-
enty-year-old virgin. They are accounts from my life and that
of my friends, my great-grandmother, Edith Wharton, and
Maya Angelou, among others.

It's important to note that obsessive love knows no age. We
often think of it as a young woman's ailment, but, sometimes,
unrequited love shows up unexpectedly a little later in life. The
unrequited story of Edith Wharton that I relay occurred when
she was forty-five. Another mature woman well acquainted

with blinding obsession was Hollywood screen goddess Marlene Dietrich. In her fifties she had it bad for actor Yul Brynner—star of *The Ten Commandments* and *The King and I*. Marlene's husband notwithstanding (he had a mistress of his own), she spent a decade enamored with Yul. The actor indulged her passion occasionally, but often left her waiting by the phone. At one point—feeling depressed and disappointed by her behavior—she wrote a letter to her good friend, playwright Noël Coward, and meekly asked, "How do I become more self-sufficient?" Noël responded with some amusingly stern advice, which I'll share in a bit.

Marlene posed a good question and one that's easy to ask in the midst of heartache. If not, "How do I become more self-sufficient?" then maybe, "How do I stop ending up in the same disheartening situation?" or "Why do I repeatedly allow the same person to bring me down?" Both the telling question and the enlightened answer lie within you. As Glinda assured Dorothy in *The Wizard of Oz*, "You've always had the power to go back to Kansas." Scarecrow was aghast at this revelation, asking, "Then why didn't you tell her before?" Glinda knew, as every parent of a teenager knows, "Because she wouldn't have believed me. She had to learn it for herself." Like Dorothy, you have the power within you the whole time; you just have to learn it for yourself. Feel free to learn from Marlene's and my mistakes along the way. We've made plenty.

As for second-grade Joey and I, we were star crossed. He moved away at the end of the school year, and I was devastated. In third grade we got a new student, Chad Baker, and the cycle started all over again.

LOVES ME...NOT

ONE

WHEN LOVE SUDDENLY APPEARS

*. . . but "falling in love" has little to do with love, and I was star-
tled to be reminded of how intoxicating it can be. The sensations
involved are, after all, undeniably delicious: not least the sensation
of being aware of risk and of a sudden release from one's
inhibitions against embracing risk. "Careful! This is likely to end
in a painful mess . . . But so what if it does!" It is exhilarating.*

—Diana Athill, *After a Funeral*

Like a shooting star interrupting the night sky or a pickup
truck running a stop sign, attraction often appears without warning. You aren't safe anywhere; it can happen while
you're at work, in the café car, sampling appetizers at Trader
Joe's, or perusing online profile pages. Sometimes it occurs,
predictably, at a bar—but it's usually on a night that you swore
you weren't going to go out. A friend inconsiderately dragged
you away from the essential task of catching up on *Downton*

Abbey season 3, and there he was—knight in a Judas Priest T-shirt—ready to rescue you from the doldrums of your life. When the sun rises the next day you tremble at the thought that you almost didn't go out. You would have missed him! Perhaps it isn't a new face you fall for but the familiar face of a friend who you are now seeing with new and excited eyes. Or maybe you're on a third date; the first two were okay, but this is the one that changes everything. Regardless of how and where, a seismic shift has taken place. A desire is born. Time is now divided between the days before and the days after he came.

Being attracted to another person is one of life's great plea- sures. It's brand new on each and every occasion—as if some- one just plugged in your senses. Sometimes it's fleeting—a smile shared between strangers at a rest stop—yet still highly enjoyable, while other times it's the beginning of something— perhaps a series of dates, a long-term relationship, or an anx- ious search for signs of reciprocation. In any case, this person, who you didn't necessarily know yesterday, becomes a focal point around which many decisions are about to be made.

The early days of a promising romance are extraordinary, free from banal burdens like gravity. I know it feels like magic but physiology does play a role. When infatuated, your brain is flooded with the neurotransmitter dopamine, which is an overseer in regions of the brain that regulate pleasure. (Dopa- mine also floods the brains of the drug addicted; in fact, rumor has it that dopamine is where heroine gets its nickname [Dope*].) In other words, you're a little high. This isn't to say

---

* According to UrbanDictionary.com: "People who do not do drugs call Marijuana Dope. People who do Marijuana call Heroin Dope."

you shouldn't enjoy the sensation. It's a natural high. Just be careful, because you haven't fallen for a person yet, you've fallen for a possibility.

There's nothing like possibility, is there? With its promise to make life much more interesting than it is right now. It's possible he'll ask me out. It's possible he'll take me to a waterfall on our first date. It's possible I'll see him with nothing but his tie on. It's possible he'll be able to navigate my body as no other can. It's possible this could all end with a Vera Wang wedding gown and a tiara on top. And who's to stop you from indulging such hope? No one. Not even the object of your daydreams. Not even he can convince you that this might not go down the way you're envisioning it.

While there's nothing wrong with letting your imagination spread her wings a bit, trouble arises when we create a fantasy and try to fit a potential partner into that scenario rather than allowing the person and situation to be what they are. This is the cornerstone of unrequited love. Somehow we go from an initial attraction to an obsession so pronounced we're willing to call it love—propelled by an active imagination and a devious neurotransmitter.

The mind can drive right past inconvenient facts, such as he's condescending to waitresses and cab drivers or you haven't heard from him in two weeks or he has a girlfriend. Your mind tells you that it's not that big of a deal, or even more dangerous, that you have the power to change these things about him. Why would a mind do this? Because it likes the feeling and doesn't want it to go away. It's similar to being at a friend's party and having a nice buzz brought on by Malibu and Pine-apple, so you up the ante to Jack and Coke to enhance the feeling. Before you know it you're peeling yourself off her bathroom floor and promising to buy her new monogrammed hand towels. You sought to sustain the feeling and somehow it went way too far.

A few times in my life I've met a man and had unrealistic visions of us ending up at the altar, the first time at age twenty-four. I knew for an absolute fact that I was going to marry this one particular guy, which made the pain more pronounced when he told me he was getting back together with his ex-girlfriend. It happened again when I was twenty-eight, and I ended up equally devastated. By the time I was in my early thirties, however, I caught on to the tricks my mind was playing on me. I went out with a handsome architect a few times and, without my permission, my mind started making plans. I said, "Okay, Brain, I can see you're doing your thing again." I concluded that this mental motion meant that I liked him, and that's all it meant. I sat back and watched my fantasies like a movie, but I didn't buy into them. I just thought, "Yes, I like him, and we'll see." When that situation didn't work out, I was disappointed but not devastated. The moral of the story is: You can be infatuated and still make sound decisions. It's like being drunk and handing your car keys to the designated driver.

YOU ARE ENTITLED TO YOUR FEELINGS

Before we worry about what's going on in Don Juan's head over there, let's get one thing straight: You are welcome to everything you're feeling. You are not out of anyone's league and you have a right to make your feelings known if that's what you choose to do. The first step, however, is to own your feelings. I realize this sounds obvious, but it's not. There is danger in admitting to yourself that you like someone, because you might be compelled to do something about it, and that means rejection becomes a possibility. Whereas if you say and do nothing, you can continue to live in a fantasy world.

This applies not just to those admiring a man from a distance but also to any woman who finds herself directly involved with a man of intrigue. If you're in a casual relationship and you want to be in a serious relationship, honor your feelings and say so. I know it's easier to pretend you just want sex, too, because by coming clean you risk losing him, even in a casual capacity. To love is to take a risk. For one, there's the risk of the other person not reciprocating. Be brave and own your feelings. He may choose to not to be involved, which is disappointing, but you will live to love again. Make sure to own your disappointment; you are entitled to that feeling as well.

In another scenario, perhaps you feel that your feelings aren't valid until the other person declares they are; maybe you subconsciously say, "My feelings don't count until he reciprocates." Then the waiting for that reciprocation begins: "Oh I'm just gonna sit here until you notice me. I'll wait until you call or text and tell me that I matter." This is like falling down the rabbit hole of unrequited love; the waiting can last for an indefinite amount of time, and the need to have him reciprocate takes on a life of its own.

End the cycle by telling yourself that you and your feelings matter. The sooner you tell yourself that your feelings are bona fide, the sooner you can decide if you're going to act on them.

If you do act and he doesn't feel the same, the sooner you can process the letdown and move on to some of life's other adventures.

THE OBJECT OF YOUR AFFECTION IS ENTITLED TO HIS FEELINGS

Now for the difficult part. The man you've set your sights on is also entitled to his feelings and those feelings may not be in your favor, and this hurts. Of course it does. The hurt, however, doesn't have to be unbearable. If you internalize his lack of interest, then yes, it's going to hurt like hell. Internalizing an amorous rejection means concluding that because someone doesn't want to be with you, you are therefore uninteresting, unattractive, and undesirable—or any other unkind words you can think of. Worse than assuming that's what the guy is thinking, you start to believe it about yourself. Then if you're anything like me, you set out to prove him wrong. Oh, I can be better. Do better. Be whoever you want me to be. You become fixated on the goal of winning his affection. With each attempt you make, and each subsequent rejection on his part, you make the ordeal last longer and you make the pain more pronounced—especially if you internalize it over and over.

The process can be significantly less painful if you focus on the truth. The truth is, "He's not romantically interested in me and that doesn't make anyone a bad person." Yes, that is the case. His lack of interest does not make you unappealing nor does it make him the scum of the earth. We are attracted to the people we're attracted to for reasons unknown—even to us. A January 2008 article in *Psychology Today* called "Scents and

Sensibility" declares, "Sexual attraction remains one of life's biggest mysteries. We might say we go for partners who are tall and thin, love to cook, or have a mania for exercise, but when push comes to shove, studies show, the people we actually end up with possess few of the traits we claim to want." While it's wonderful when two people share an attraction, initially it's good fortune. *You like me? Well, what do you know! I like you too!* If the relationship moves forward, it then becomes less happenstance and more hard work, but at first it's just chance and therefore nothing to internalize if someone isn't interested.

When I was a freshman in college I ended up in earshot of an unreciprocated confession at a party one night. Rose—a girl who lived on my dorm floor—was confessing her love to Jack. Most of the girls on our floor had a crush on Jack, myself included, but Rose was outwardly determined in her pursuit of him. The two were friends and that's as far as he wanted it to go. I overheard them while I was in line for the bathroom. "What do you want me to do?" she was saying. "I'll do anything. Do you want me to take my shirt off right now? What do you want me to do?" Many college boys would have gladly taken her up on that offer. He, mercifully, did not. Instead he repeated himself solemnly, "Please don't do this. Please don't do this." It seemed to me that he was trying to avoid hurting her. By no one's fault they felt differently about each other. She thought him not liking her made her less of a person, and so she begged for his approval and sulked—in a big chair in the corner—when she didn't get it.

Now, it would be nice if all men clearly stated, "I appreciate the offer but I don't feel the same way you do." Oh, but they don't. Oftentimes they prefer to be vague so they can sleep with you, have you come over when they are bored or lonely, or even borrow money in some interesting cases. As much as we wish they wouldn't do this, they do. You can protect yourself by owning your feelings and being honest about them—not bending your will at the wave of his hand. If he responds negatively to what you want, then respect his feelings and start to let go.

If you love someone—there is no possible harm in saying so . . . It sometimes happens that what you feel is not returned for one reason or another—but that does not make your feeling less valuable and good.

—John Steinbeck, author of *Grapes of Wrath* and *Of Mice and Men*, in a sweet letter to his son fourteen-year-old son, Thom, in 1958

WISDOM OF A POP STAR

This is my friend Elizabeth's story, and I share it with permission. Elizabeth and her girlfriends were in Puerto Rico for a bachelorette weekend. While leaving a restaurant in Old San Juan one evening, they spotted a celebrity. Timberlake. Justin Timberlake. As JT exited the building and walked toward his car, one of the girls asked if they could have their picture taken with him. He made eye contact, said nothing, and got in the car—with the windows conveniently down. Like a good bachelorette, Elizabeth dutifully shouted, "Diiiick!" The car, which had started to pull away, stopped. JT got out and said, "Did you just call me a dick? I'm not a dick because you didn't get what you want!" He makes an excellent point.

It is certifiably impossible to please all people, all of the time. An international celebrity knows this very well, and we civilians have our experience with it, too. Mr. Timberlake's candid statement applies directly to unrequited attraction. It's tempting to make Mr. Would-Be-Right a bad guy simply because you aren't getting what you want; when in reality he hasn't done anything wrong. You can't please everyone all the time and neither can your heartthrob. If his only "crime" is not having the same level of interest that you have, he's not a dick. Don't get me wrong, there is *plenty* of behavior that makes a guy a dick, which we'll discuss, but he doesn't owe you anything just because you exist. Humbling, yet true.

As for the bride-to-be and her gaggle of girls, Elizabeth apologized and JT stood for what is probably one of the greatest bachelorette photos ever. When Elizabeth posted the pic on Facebook she wrote, "What's up now bc we SO got what we wanted!!!! Best time ever!!!!!!" It worked out in this case because Justin didn't have to commit to more than a 30-second pose. Keep in mind it doesn't always go down like this.

PRESENTING YOUR CASE

So let's say you've established that you have feelings of the passionate kind for some local lady-killer. To do or not to do something about them—that is the question. You may've thought of everything I've thought of to probe your crush. You can friend him on Facebook. Invite him to coffee. Ask him out for a drink if you're feeling especially daring. Carry his books home from school. Slip a pair of Tiffany's oval cufflinks—sterling silver with white-enamel finish—in his locker. I've done them all. I can say with certainty that men prefer to do the asking—yes, still in the twenty-first century—but we women have come so far in every other gender-related capacity that most of us can't bear the thought of doing *nothing*.

I say do something small—cast a flirtatious line in his direction. Make a minor move so you feel secure in the fact that you put your attraction out into the ether. If you do this, be willing to take no, or no response, for an answer. Otherwise you can easily convince yourself that your gesture was too small. Then you end up making a series of attempts—becoming more determined with each one.

On the other side of things, if you're nervous about the potential rejection, ask yourself what you're afraid of. Are you scared of the rejection itself or the fact that you can't keep the fantasy going if he says no? Sometimes an illusion feels like the safest place to be. If you don't want to nudge him, that's fine, but I encourage you not to hold on to the idea of him too tightly. If you keep watching from a distance and saying, "As soon as he notices me . . . just as soon as he notices . . ." you can get caught in that cerebral spin cycle and find yourself completely obsessed without any suggestive interaction with him.

Personally, I've always been more afraid of regret than rejection. Between the ages of eighteen and twenty-eight I was forthright, shall we say, in my pursuit of certain members of the male gender. My instincts told me that it was best to do everything I possibly could to make my feelings known so that I'll never wonder "What would have happened if . . ." Looking back, I'm amused that this was my gut feeling. I've made a fool of myself countless times, but I don't wonder what would have happened. *I* know.

Now that I'm past that brazen decade of my life, I've come to appreciate that you can still make your intentions known without going to extremes. You can give something an honest attempt and walk away—if need be—with your head held high. The key is to walk away—rather than taking the "If I have to lie, steal, cheat, or kill, as God as my witness, I WILL have that man," approach.

For those who find it difficult to back down, I understand the feeling, because chasing a crush can feel noble. You convince yourself that you're going out on a limb for love and how dare anyone try to stop you. But consider this: part of what you're chasing is the fantasy you've created. You've placed all your bets on this idea of him, and you don't want to lose. You want to win so badly you overlook the fact that he's not looking. You're afraid to give up the chase because it feels like giving up on love. I assure you it's not. It's giving up on the idea of this person. Love is still out there, and if you can tear yourself away from this guy, you stand a better chance of finding it.

I will gladly share some of my forthright stories in these pages, but first I'll tell you what I have come to believe a sensible pursuit looks like: It is a balance between putting yourself out there and accepting a less-than-desirable outcome and not going too far. During my first semester in grad school—at the age of thirty-three—I formed a classroom crush; I had instant visions of my new weekend wardrobe made up of his colorful array of hoodies. It seemed that he—let's call him James T. Kirk—had a modicum of interest, too. He'd wait for me after class sometimes, and if he came in late—as he often did—he'd make a point to wave and smile when he sat down. I friended

him on Facebook. He accepted the request but did no more, so
I shrugged my shoulders.

A few weeks later, James and I ended up having a long conversation after class. I asked him if he wanted to continue it
over coffee. We went to a nearby café and within the hour he
asked me if I wanted to go out. Score! He took my number and
I floated home. Several days went by and there was no word
from him. We had class together again on Wednesday and he
said hello but acted distant—as if our conversation on Saturday
had never taken place. I was confused, let down, and nervous
about having to see him again twice a week for the next few
months. It's either very brave or very foolish to blow someone
off when you see her bi-weekly.

It wasn't necessarily awkward the next few times we saw
each other; we just didn't go out of our way to speak as we had
before. Eventually everything was fine; fine because I went to
the greatest place there is—the island of not giving a damn. I
decided not to ask what happened because if he'd wanted to
explain, he would have. He knew what he did was inconsiderate—that's why he was being distant. I wasn't about to remind
him that he had asked me out; we both know he did. Ultimately, we went back to being cordial classmates. I was pleased
that I put my interest out there in a modest way and I was,
understandably, frustrated with his rudeness. I recognized,
however, that that's all it was—rude. His blowing me off wasn't
going to start a nuclear holocaust. I was able to move past it
quickly because I accepted his action at face value and went
right back to studying. At first he was a nice distraction from
class. In the end, class was the perfect distraction from him. As

mentioned, this wouldn't always have been my chosen route—
more to come on how I determined that walking away is the
best course of action.

DON'T BUILD AN ENTIRE LIFE AROUND
A FEW ENCOUNTERS

Naturally, there are times when the guy asks for your number
and he really does call. You go out once, twice, maybe even
three times, and find yourself completely smitten. Conversation
is easy and kissing is electric. Surely now it's okay to start laying
the concrete foundation for your brownstone in Brooklyn? Not
just yet. By all means enjoy yourself and savor every moment,
but do just that—savor the present moment. Take it one date at
a time. Let things unfold slowly. Let him demonstrate his interest in you before you grant him the gift of your lifelong loyalty. It's vital, too, to figure out if there's a genuine connection
on your side versus deciding that he's going to fit perfectly into
your already existing plans.

If it's the third date and you find yourself choosing your
kids' names, you've started future tripping. Yes, that's right—
the future is a drug, and it's hazardous to your mental health.
You may imagine that your life will be so much better in the
future and you ignore what's happening around you. In es-
sence, you neglect to live your life because you're so focused on
what comes next.

This is how it plays out: suppose you've gone out on three
dates with a guy but haven't heard from him about making a
fourth. You suffer not just from the loss of him but the loss of

your future together. You made all these plans; the two of you were going to go to Nantucket for the weekend, and you were going to introduce him to all your friends. He was going to propose in Turks and Caicos! Now you're let down that those things aren't going to happen—except there was no real indication that it was going to happen in the first place. Your mind went off on its own adventure and forgot to bring reality.

Future tripping can be an endless rotation because if you get to the future and you don't like it, you just project your mind further into the future where things *really will* be perfect this time. You can live your whole life anticipating what is going to happen when—when I get a new job, when I get married, when we have children, when my house looks like the Crate & Barrel catalog—rather than paying attention to the "now."

Have fun while dating, but try not to skip ahead. Stay present, whether it's the fourth date, fourth month, or fourth year. There's no downside to doing this. If things don't work out, it will be easier to let go. If things do work out and the two of you end up together, the future still isn't going to be exactly what you imagine. The more you build it up, the more it can let you down, and you might unfairly blame the man. After each date, say to yourself, "That was fun (amazing, tremendous, wild, adjective of your choice). I hope to see him again." Then take a deep breath and delight in the moment.

If you haven't had at least a slight poetic crack in the heart, you have been cheated by nature.

—Phyllis Battelle

FORGET THE FAIRYTALES AND THE "GREATEST" LOVE STORY OF ALL TIME

It's no secret where these cockamamie fantasies about the flaw-less future come from. Even before we can speak in complete sentences we are introduced to a world where animals sing fal-setto and princes are the solution to every problem. While we eventually accept that mice don't make the best confidants, it's more difficult to let go of the prince and the promise of some-day. You just aren't there yet. Your problems haven't been solved because the person who is going to solve them hasn't shown up yet. But he will show up, and when he does, your life will fi-nally have meaning. This is the first of many fairytale false-hoods.

Another one of the major fairytale misrepresentations is where the story ends: The wedding. The villain is dead and the entire kingdom celebrates. Then Aladdin and Jasmine fly off on their magic carpet and Ariel and Eric sail into the sunset. This makes it appear as though the wedding is the finish line. Once you get there, you've made it. The difficult part is over. In real life, the work hasn't even begun. The wedding is the start-ing block. It's the beginning of a marathon relationship and it takes serious effort to keep up.

After the wedding, of course, the pair lives happily ever after. This concept implies that there will come a day when misery can no longer touch you. It's part of what keeps us fo-cused on the future and chasing that elusive relationship. Once x, y, and z happen, then I won't have to deal with sorrow any-more. It will be nothing but happiness from there on out. In truth, there is no amount of money, no level of fame, and no romantic liaison that will stop you from ever being sad. It sounds like bad news, but it doesn't have to be. By accepting that you're going to feel down sometimes—that it's a natural part of the life cycle—you won't be upset when you can't maintain constant joy. You'll understand your emotions come and go like seasons regardless of relationship status.

Once we're done with the first decade of life—the decade of Disney cartoons—we enter adolescence and what awaits us there is another set of misguided love stories that come in the form of required high school reading. Enter stage right: William Shakespeare—he who speaks the language of love. It's been suggested that *Romeo and Juliet* is the greatest love story of all time. I don't mean to be a downer, but it's the tale of two teenagers who kill themselves after knowing each other less than a week. The play begins on Sunday and the star-crossed lovers take their lives on Thursday. Are we condoning this? Not to mention the play opens with Romeo post rejection. He's pining after a girl named Rosaline, who turned him down. He goes to the Capulet ball hoping to run into Roz and he meets Juliet instead. So Jules is essentially a rebound, and it appears as though Romeo will pant over any pretty Capulet girl.

Next up we have *Hamlet*. In this play there is lovely ingénue named Ophelia who falls for a man who really likes to talk to himself—Hamlet, Prince of Denmark. He rejects her, humiliates her, and kills her father. She tragically drowns a short while later. Is it any wonder we declare our lives are over when love doesn't work out the way we want it to?

These are two versions of romantic love presented to us as our minds are developing—absolute perfection or unbearable tragedy. When high school is over, romantic comedies, jewelry ads, and the wedding industry pick right up where the fairytales left off. They perpetuate the original idea of the perfect day and the perfect person while adding a few new fables to the mix such as, *The Nuclear Family Is the Right Family* and *I Am Incomplete Until Someone Else Completes Me.* So we sit and look ahead to "someday," feeling inadequate if we haven't arrived.

THE THREE WISE MEN

That's it. I've had enough. I'm breaking up with Walt D. and Will S. Why? They play too many head games. Disney is always making promises he can't keep, and Shakespeare is a drama queen. I'm done—for good this time. There are some new men in my life and I'd like to introduce you to them. They've given me a whole new outlook on love, and I'll refer to them throughout the rest of this book.

The first object of my affection is dead (then again so are Walt and Will), but his words are alive and his wisdom is such a turn on. His name is Erich Fromm (1900–1980), as mentioned in the Introduction. Born in Germany, Fromm was a psychoanalyst, psychologist, and sociologist. He wrote many books, but the one I'm going to focus on is called *The Art of Loving.* Written in 1956, this bestselling book dispels the idea that love is supernatural and inexplicable. One of the first fairytale notions that Fromm denounces is the idea of "The One." We believe that love begins when one singular sensation of a man walks in the room and that the purpose of love is to adore him above all others. But Fromm says something different; he suggests that love—even romantic love—needs to be all-inclusive: "If a person loves only one other person and is indifferent to the rest of his fellow men, his love is not love but a symbiotic attachment, or an enlarged egotism . . . If I truly love one person I love all persons, I love the world, I love life."

Another guy that I'm crushing on is Eckhart Tolle, born in 1948, also in Germany. You may have heard of him—he's been on *Oprah*. In his book *The Power of Now: A Guide to Spiritual Enlightenment* he stresses that many of life's problems come from a preoccupation with the past and the future. Our inability to live in the present moment, according to Tolle, keeps us from peace and joy. What does this have to do with unrequited love? Everything. We've already discussed a few ways in which the future can impair our vision, but the past does its damage, too. As unrequited lovers we are constantly replaying memories of when we were with that special someone. In unrequited love, we want to be anywhere but here—yesterday when I was in his arms or tomorrow when I'll make him love me again. Tolle tells us that freedom from obsession lies in living in the moment. He, like Fromm, takes the idea of love beginning when the right person comes along and turns it on its head. On the contrary, he says, love begins right now: "Your love is not outside; it is deep within you. You can never lose it, and it cannot leave you. It is not dependent on some other body, some external form."

The last man I'm inviting to my enlightened foursome is Don Miguel Ruiz, born in 1952 in Mexico. He is most well-known for his book *The Four Agreements: A Practical Guide to Personal Wisdom*, which I'll reference, but I also want to focus on a lesser known, equally poignant work of his called *The*

Mastery of Love: A Practical Guide to the Art of Relationship.
These three men come from different educational and spiritual
backgrounds yet their insights on love are remarkably similar.
Ruiz expands on Tolle's notion that love starts within. He says
not only does love start with you, but it cannot exist without
you. In *The Mastery of Love* he plainly states, "You cannot share
what you do not have. If you do not love yourself, you cannot
love anyone else either." I had always thought love was completely contingent on another person. Isn't this interesting? It
makes unrequited love a blessing in disguise—giving us a
chance to get that self-love thing squared away before doing
anything else.

TWO

WHEN LOVE SUDDENLY DISAPPEARS

He slept a summer by my side
He filled my days with endless wonder
He took my childhood in his stride
But he was gone when autumn came
—From the song "I Dreamed a Dream," from the musical
Les Miserables, English lyrics by Herbert Kretzmer

As suddenly and inexplicably as passion begins, it can end. One day the phone calls and text messages become distressingly spaced out. When you do talk, something isn't right. You can't quite put your finger on it, but you know this behavior pales in comparison to the way it was before. You ask if something's wrong. He says everything is fine—if he says anything at all; he might've simply disappeared, leaving only silence.

A girlfriend of mine fell in love for the first time at the age of seventeen with a man whose last name was—I kid you not—Casanova. All was blissful for six months. They spoke every weekday at the same time in the early evening. One night she called him and the phone rang and rang. This was in the prehistoric days before cell phones and he did not have an answering machine. She called him every day for a week only to be confronted with the same endless ringing. She wasn't sure what to feel first—hurt, confusion, or worry. Eventually she had no choice but to accept that it was over. A year later she ran into him and asked what had happened. He, surely squirming in his skin, said he couldn't handle her going away to college. I believe the logic (illogic) here is, "I don't want to hurt her feelings, so I just won't say anything." I wonder if, in the years since, he's ever been on the other side of that situation. Only then could he understand the agony of knowing nothing. The mind oscillates back and forth between fear that something terrible has happened and excruciating pain not only because the relationship is over but that someone who seemed to care chose to end things in such a heartless way.

It's not just new romances that end irresponsibly. Sometimes long-term love ends this way, too. In early 1920, after seventeen years of marriage, my great-grandfather, Russell, left his wife (my great-grandmother), Winifred, and their children. He disappeared and was never heard from again. Although they never legally divorced, we now know that he married another woman and had a family with her. Under those circumstances, I'm not sure which would be more hurtful—the not knowing or the knowing. Both are abhorrent. Six years after he left, Winifred died of uterine cancer at the age of forty-nine.

I think of her sometimes. I wonder if there was a moment she knew he was never coming back or if she found herself looking at the door hoping to see him. I wonder if she thought of him every day for the rest of her life. She must have. I think of him, too, and wonder, What the hell precedes a decision like that? How can you enjoy the beginnings of a new family as if you don't already have children wondering where you are?

The descendants of Russell's first family (my family) have since been in touch with the descendants of his second family and we are piecing together the puzzle. The silver lining of the story is that Winifred was able to provide love and stability for her children despite her husband's disappearance. My grandfather, David, and his siblings, my great-Uncle Robert, Aunt Betty, and Uncle Ollie were able to go on and have successful lives—personally and professionally. They spoke highly of their mother and her enduring strength all their lives.

Whether a man disappears after two seemingly fun dates, six months, or seventeen years, the mind goes into creative overdrive—grabbing onto any excuse it can. I don't mean to liken someone disappearing after less than a year to one who disappears after almost two decades; I'm simply saying that in each case a man walks away and it causes pain. In the end, you can't measure your pain against someone else's; you can't convince a seventeen-year-old—or anyone—who thinks her world has ended that her world hasn't actually ended. She only knows what she feels and that it hurts. A loss has been experienced, and denial is a significant stage of grief—hence the excuses we tend to make. He must be . . . overwhelmed, afraid, in a ditch, or kidnapped by Russian spies. The situation must be something other than what it appears to be. It isn't really over. This isn't actually happening. Moving on depends on how long the denial lasts.

Forgotten you? —Well if forgetting
Be thinking all day
How long hours drag since you left me
Days seem years with you away
If the wild wish to see you and hear you
To be held in your arms again
If this be forgetting, I'm wrong
And I have forgotten you then.

—Anonymous

WHAT'S WRONG WITH ME?

Regardless of how the object of our affection leaves—with an actual breakup or the silent slip away—we find ourselves begging the question; "What's wrong with me?" Let the self-interrogation begin: *But what's wrong with me? I'm nice, aren't I? I'm cute, right? Is it my credit score? But it's 745! And my carbon footprint is, like, nonexistent. Is it my Jessica Simpson perfume? I'll never wear it again!*

This question is the panic button. We scramble to figure out what we're doing, saying, wearing incorrectly. Here's the crazy part: We're willing to change it all. We ask what we're doing wrong so we can hurry up, fix it, and get this guy back onboard. That wouldn't be a problem except IT'S THE EXACT OPPOSITE OF LOVE. The whole point is to find someone who adores you as you already are—flaws and all. I'm guessing you have some personality defects, several bad habits, maybe a handful of insecurities. I have those, too. So do married people. So does Kate Middleton. So does this guy you're crazy about. It doesn't make any of us unworthy of love.

I once asked a guy what was wrong with me. We had been seeing each other for a few weeks and I had never known anything to be off to such a good start. Then one night I found myself on the phone swallowing tears—he was getting back together with his ex. I meekly asked, "Did I do something wrong?" He responded, "No, you have been wonderful." Somehow that didn't help. It didn't change what was happening. I clung to the words anyway. He thinks I'm wonderful! Of course, he was long gone and I was still soothing myself with those empty words.

Let's say that guy didn't use the word *wonderful*. Let's say he used the word *worthless* instead. It would have shattered me, and I would have lost sleep wondering, "How do I become worthy?" I have since learned that the answer lies in not leaving my personal value up to him—or anyone. I can't fix myself according to him because what that guy sees is just that, what he sees. It doesn't mean another man won't see the exact same quirks, find them charming, and want to stick around to enjoy them.

In September 2011 a woman named Sara Eckel wrote an essay for *The New York Times*. The story opens as a man she's on a date with asks how long it's been since her last relationship. She evades the question—afraid to admit she hadn't been in a serious relationship in eight years. Many dates before this one, she did answer the question. Her date cringed and asked, "What's wrong with you?" Sara then excused herself early and went home to sulk—it was a question she presented to herself many times.

By asking yourself, "What's wrong with me?" you are giving one man (or several men) the power to determine your self-worth. That's an awful lot of power over your life. Sure you want to give it away? By all means be sad that a relationship has ended or that it isn't officially beginning as you had hoped, but try not to let it shake your core. One way to do this is by refusing to ask yourself the degrading question in the first place. Instead say, "I gave it my best shot and it didn't work out. I am open to loving and being loved in return. It hasn't happened yet. That's all." And trust that the universe knows something you don't: there's someone you're even more compatible with out there.

The man Sara was on a date with at the beginning of the essay turned out to be a keeper. They dated for a month before she confessed how long it had been since she'd been serious with someone. When she did, he didn't care. He went so far as to declare himself lucky and say the men who turned her down were fools. Mark and Sara are now married. And that's how it will be. When a quality partner is looking, what's wrong with you will pale in comparison to what's right with you.

DON'T TAKE IT (OR ANYTHING) PERSONALLY

In the last chapter I mentioned the practice of internalizing— assuming another person's behavior is a direct reflection of you and going on to believe it about yourself. The more common way to say this is "taking it personally." We humans are very quick to take things personally. Your brother forgets your birthday, the boss singles you out at the Monday meeting, or a friend writes an inconsiderate comment on Facebook and you let it get you down for the rest of the day.

Since we take minor things so personally, it's nearly impossible for us not to take breakups personally. In intimate relationships we get naked—literally and figuratively—and therefore we absorb the rejection into our very being. We let it sink deep into our souls and change the way we see ourselves. Yet, as unnecessary as it is to ask yourself, "What's wrong with me?" it's unnecessary to take a relationship that doesn't work out personally. It's unnecessary to take anything personally. It's incredibly difficult but still unnecessary.

In 1997, Don Miguel Ruiz had his first book published: *The Four Agreements: A Practical Guide to Personal Wisdom*. The book is simple in language and profound in concept. The Four Agreements are:

1. **Be Impeccable with Your Word**—Speak with integrity. Say only what you mean. Avoid using the Word to speak against yourself or to gossip about others. Use the power of your Word in the direction of truth and love.

2. **Don't Take Anything Personally**—Nothing others do is because of you. What others say and do is a projection of their own reality, their own dream. When you are immune to the opinions and actions of others, you won't be the victim of needless suffering.

3. **Don't Make Assumptions**—Find the courage to ask questions and to express what you really want. Communicate with others as clearly as you can to avoid misunderstandings, sadness, and drama.

4. **Always Do Your Best**—Your best is going to change from moment to moment; it will be different when you are healthy as opposed to sick. Under any circumstance, simply do your best and you will avoid self-judgment, self-abuse, and regret.

Each of these agreements is powerful. We're going to zero in on number two. Let's say your boyfriend breaks up with you and is in another relationship within a week. The breakup hits the left side of your face and his new relationship smashes the right. You ache because what he's saying with his actions is that she's better than you. Is she really better than you or is he so terrified of spending a Saturday night alone that he'll take whoever comes along? Or perhaps he, too, is feeling tender and vulnerable (like our good friend Romeo) and she just happens to be there. If, according to him, she is "better" than you, ask yourself what that means exactly. Maybe she can do more jumping jacks. Or perhaps she can change a tire faster. My point? The idea of someone or something being "better" is completely subjective; that's why we must never be bothered to take things personally.

We are all walking around the planet looking at each other through the lens of our own insecurities and fears. Everyone has a subconscious agenda he or she is advancing. People may not like you for reasons that have nothing to do with you. Even if someone walks right up to you and says, "I hate you!" you are not the problem. That person's need to spew hate is the problem. If you take it personally, you'll suffer and most likely spew it right back. Otherwise, you'll walk away unscathed and forget it.

It's important, also, to be aware of our own tendency to express dislike for others. We judge people based on our psychological shortcomings; noticing other people's blemishes is being self-conscious about our own. If you find it frustrating when people cancel plans at the last minute or speak in an obnoxiously loud voice in public, you might be guilty of doing the same. If you are careful not to do these things and it still noticeably bothers you when others do, it is likely the problem originates with you in another way. For example, your frenemy in junior high canceled plans with you often to hang out with the cool crowd or your overcritical mother speaks too loudly in restaurants. You're subconsciously reminded of these past upsets when people do them in the present.

By not taking things personally, it doesn't mean you don't care about others; it just means that you no longer allow their insecurities to trigger your insecurities. You no longer assume people vote Republican just to piss you off. You see what others say and do as an outward expression of what's going on inside them rather than a reflection of you. In this scenario, even my great-grandmother could've opted not to take her husband leaving personally. I'm sure she did, who wouldn't? For argument's sake, however, let's say she'd been a good wife and mother for the seventeen years they were together—I'm confident she was, considering that she was a good mother after he left. Let's also say that the midlife crisis (or whatever) took place in his mind. He reacted to the voices in his head telling him he hadn't done enough with his life or that another woman would make his demons go away. In that case, *he* would've been the reason he left, not she.

While it's a splendid concept, not taking things personally isn't easy to practice—especially if you, like me, have been taking things personally all your life. Start small—give it a try the next time a coworker makes a careless comment. Eventually, work your way up to friends and family and aim to ultimately apply it to Prince Charming. The times I've managed to accept that another's behavior has nothing to do with me have felt like absolute freedom. The opposite—when I realize that a problem I'm having is mine alone and I can stop blaming others for it—is liberating, too. From *The Four Agreements*:

"Whatever happens around you, don't take it personally. . . . Nothing other people do is because of you. It is because of themselves. All people live in their own dream, in their own mind; they are in a completely different world from the one we live in. When we take something personally, we make the assumption that they know what is in our world, and we try to impose our world on their world.

"Even when a situation seems so personal, even if others insult you directly, it has nothing to do with you. What they say, what they do, and the opinions they give are according to the agreements they have in their own minds. They can hook you easily with one little opinion and feed you whatever poison they want, and because you take it personally, you eat it up . . .

"When we really see other people as they are without taking it personally, we can never be hurt by what they say or do. Even if others lie to you, it is okay. They are lying to you because they are afraid . . .

"When you make it a strong habit not to take anything personally, you avoid many upsets in your life. Your anger, jealousy, and envy will disappear, and even your sadness will simply disappear if you don't take anything personally."

SINGING IN THE RAIN OF REJECTION

At first sight, unrequited love appears to be a wretched, gloomy, miserable state to be stuck in. Your ideal mate has turned you down. But instead of asking yourself dejectedly, "What am I going to do now?" present yourself with a new question: "What aren't I going to do?" You are equipped to climb Mount Kilimanjaro, start a small business, write a novel, or learn to play the cello. You just lost the thing you thought you wanted most in the world. What do you have to lose now? Nothing. Life has handed you an opportunity to become a master of rejection. I highly recommend you take it.

Life is full of rejection—personal and professional. Lilacs don't grow without rain and humans don't grow without rejection. If you accept one major setback as confirmation that you are incompetent and never attempt anything worthwhile again, then you will avoid future rejection. However, you will also avoid success. There will never come a day when rejection isn't a possibility. As with sadness, no amount of money or fame can spare you. In fact those elements make it worse because then your humiliation is front-page news. The business deal can fall through. The Oscar can go to someone else. The audience can boo you off stage. The critics can write a scathing review. Your last movie may have been a blockbuster and your next one might be *Gigli*. If you accept that as evidence of your own ineptitude and give up, then you aren't going to make *Argo*, the 2012 Academy Award–winning Best Picture.

In 1976 Steve Jobs cofounded Apple Computer Company. Nine years later Apple's board of directors removed him as manager of the Macintosh Division. Wouldn't you just give up? Seriously, the company you *cofounded* gave you the shaft. Instead, Jobs went on to found NeXT, Inc. In 1996 Apple asked Jobs to come back to the tune of purchasing NeXT for $427 million. In 2005, he gave a speech at Stanford University and referenced that time in his life. He said, "I didn't see it then, but it turned out that getting fired from Apple was the best thing that could have ever happened to me. The heaviness of being successful was replaced by the lightness of being a beginner again, less sure about everything. It freed me to enter one of the most creative periods of my life. . . . I'm pretty sure none of this would have happened if I hadn't been fired from Apple. It was awful-tasting medicine, but I guess the patient needed it."

Part of longing to be in a relationship is wanting to be done with the days of romantic rejection. Don't be too hasty, however. Once you're in a committed relationship, the rejection associated with dating—such as guys not calling—might be in the rear-view mirror, but new and exciting types of rejection lie ahead. There's small rejection (you'll snub each other's choice of curtains) and rejection that hurts more (like turning down each other's sexual advances). If you take every rebuff to mean there's something terribly wrong with you or the relationship, there will be regular unrest. But if you can shake off some of the innocuous rejection—knowing it's par for the commitment course—you can more easily tell the difference between a bruised ego and a genuine problem.

Fortunately, unrequited love is preparing you to become a rejection ninja. A few steps to sharpen your skills:

1. Allow yourself the time to feel bad about things that didn't work out—don't rush through this. It's okay to feel let down.
2. If you made a mistake, don't criticize yourself. Call it just that—a mistake. (We *all* make mistakes sometimes.)
3. Recognize that the failure of things to work out isn't a reflection of your self-worth or abilities.
4. Find a lesson or three that can be taken away from the situation.
5. Put your black turtleneck on and get back out there.

THE BENEFITS OF BEING ALONE

An observer by nature, in my mid-twenties I started to notice the role fear can play in relationships. Fear is the other four-letter emotion that governs so many of our decisions. I noticed some of my friends wouldn't break up with a boyfriend until they had another suitor waiting in the wings. One girlfriend of mine was in a highly contentious relationship; there seemed to be little joy and endless fighting. She and her boyfriend started berating each other six months in and didn't stop until they broke up three years later. Even when it was girl's night out, she was often in the corner on the phone arguing with him. Eventually, I realized that though the relationship was in a constant state of upheaval she thought the alternative—being alone—was just too terrible to bear.

My guy friends appeared to have the same issue, but it manifested in a different way. They weren't always in relationships, but they had to be loosely dating someone. They wanted a girl

waiting by the phone—even if it was someone they didn't profess to like all that much.

I often marveled at the upkeep these not-so-great relationships required—wondering why go through it if the core bond
itself isn't solid or satisfying. In the privacy of my own mind I
started to think, Maybe it's okay to be alone. Maybe it's even . . .
necessary to know yourself in this way. I usually dismissed that
view—figuring I was just trying to make myself feel better for
having lousy luck in love. Then one day someone else made the
same suggestion. Elizabeth Gilbert wrote in her smash hit *Eat,
Pray, Love*, "I got started early in life with pursuit of sexual and
romantic pleasure. I barely had an adolescence before I had my
first boyfriend, and I have consistently had a boy or man (or
sometimes both) in my life ever since I was fifteen years old.
That was—oh, let's see—about nineteen years ago, now. That's
almost two solid decades I have been entwined in some kind of
drama with some kind of guy. Each overlapping the next, with
never so much as a week's breather in between. And I can't
help but think that's been something of a liability on my path
to maturity."

Years later, I was reading *The Art of Loving* and Erich
Fromm takes it a step further by saying the fear of being alone
not only stifles maturity but love itself. "If I am attached to
another person because I cannot stand on my own two feet, he
or she may be a lifesaver, but the relationship is not one of love.
Paradoxically, the ability to be alone is the condition for the
ability to love." Eckhart Tolle says it, too: "If you cannot be at
ease with yourself when you are alone, you will seek a relationship to cover up your unease. You can be sure that the unease
will reappear in some other form within the relationship and

you will probably hold your partner responsible for it." And
not to be left out, Don Miguel Ruiz is also on board. In *The
Mastery of Love* he writes, "You are complete. When love is
coming out of you, you are not searching for love because you
are afraid to be alone. When you have all that love for yourself,
you can be alone and there's no problem. You are happy to be
alone, and to share is also fun."

How can being alone be the condition for love? When you
enter into a relationship, you give yourself to another person,
but in order to do so you must have a self to give. If you're afraid
to be alone, you cannot give. You can only cling. You cling to
another person and steal your identity from him, and if he
goes, so goes your identity. Then, much of the agony is not just
the end of the relationship but also the loss of the only sense of
self you have. Whereas if your sense of self is yours—and yours
alone—anyone leaving your life can be disruptive and disappointing, but it won't be the end of your world. You can even be
the one to walk away if you feel a situation isn't right.

Being alone is also an opportunity to face some of your insecurities. We mistakenly think romantic relationships are
going to solve our psychological problems. The relationship
may mask issues for a while, but they always resurface. For
example, suppose you feel unattractive in some way and think
that having a boyfriend will prove to the world that you're one-
hundred-percent beautiful. I know women with body issues
who are married to very attractive men. Did marrying a hot
guy cure them of those issues? Nope. They still speak openly
about not liking their bodies. Their husbands tell them they're
gorgeous, which eases the anxiety for a minute or two, but the

overarching self-consciousness remains. Only they can learn to love their bodies—no one else can do it for them.

A team of researchers at Michigan State University led by psychologist Richard E. Lucas, Ph.D., have studied the effect marriage has on overall happiness. They conclude that people often experience an upgrade in happiness following their nuptials—said to last about two years—but they ultimately return to their standard levels of happiness—or unhappiness. Essentially you will walk on air for a while in a new relationship and think there will never be another cloudy day, but dopamine levels eventually return to normal. When they do, you may think that something has gone wrong with your relationship. You used to feel happy all the time and now you no longer do. If you've spent time by yourself and are well acquainted with your regular range of emotion, this won't catch you off guard. You will slide more easily into the less-euphoric portion of the program. If you've never spent time alone, though, you'll likely have a harder time with it.

Yes, it's true: contrary to popular belief, marriage is not a never-ending trip to Disney World. Married life can be quiet and routine. Anyone who has trouble being still and enjoying life's simple pleasures may seek excitement outside of the relationship or create unnecessary drama within it. Accepting life for what it is rather than what you think it should be will prepare you well, in general, for marriage and for life.

Naturally, being alone after a breakup is painful. Many assume that being alone is that painful all the time, which motivates the rush into the next liaison. I encourage you to wait through that period of distress. Spend time with your friends and family, and slowly incorporate a few hours, maybe even an entire afternoon, of being by yourself. Don't put your dating profile back online just yet. Wait until you can be in your own presence and feel not just okay, but satisfied. Try on a new frame of mind—instead of thinking "I'm pathetic," allow yourself to feel empowered. Your ability to do this is going to improve all of your relationships—romantic and otherwise. The day will come when dating feels like a choice rather than an absolute must. Then put your profile back online—if you want—or be by yourself until you meet someone in another capacity.

> *Many people suffer from the fear of finding oneself alone, and so they don't find themselves at all.*
>
> —Rollo May, *Man's Search for Himself*

DON'T GIVE ME THAT "BEING ALONE" CRAP

A few years ago I had an e-mail exchange with a girlfriend on the topic of being single. She expressed something I think many would agree with: "I mean, the idea that we're supposed to be this island unto ourselves is great, but I remember how happy I was when I was in a relationship, it really is great. It's a wonderful thing. My therapist wanted me to feel OK with being alone, but really, why can't we just own up to the fact that it's lacking otherwise. Since we were little we've dreamt of meeting a great partner, because it's great being with someone that cares about you and you them. It just is."

Her point of view is valid and, again, one I believe is shared by many. This is my response: You are the only guarantee you have. You are the only person you are going to wake up with every single day of your life. Anyone else can leave you at any time for any reason—good, bad, or tragic. This isn't something to be afraid of, it's just something to know. The same way you know winter is coming. If someone ran up to you in the middle of July in panic mode and said, "Winter is coming! What are we going to do?!" you would explain that winter isn't coming *tomorrow*, but we'll deal with it when it gets here. You can know that winter (or hurricane season if you live in a tropical climate) is coming without letting it spoil your summer the same way you can know relationships will inevitably change. Even couples that stay together for life go through difficult, uncertain periods. If you have a good relationship with yourself, you will be the mountain—steady and strong—while the seasons change all around you. Otherwise you are at the mercy of the wind.

Being okay with being alone doesn't mean you no longer desire romance or love; it just means you recognize that there are some things only you can do for you. You can love the people in your life more fully if you put your emotional oxygen mask on first, which includes making authentic relationship decisions instead of fear-based ones. If you consider being alone an exercise that will enable you to love more genuinely and be better prepared when a sudden tornado comes through, it doesn't sound so bad anymore, does it?

MY PASSION VS. HIS DALLIANCE

Edith Wharton (1862–1937) had a difficult marriage. Her husband, Edward (Teddy) Robbins Wharton, twelve years her senior, was emotionally unstable and actively unfaithful. It's difficult to know if they considered themselves to be in love. Married in 1885 when she was twenty-three, they both came from well-established families and were expected to find socially significant spouses. On their wedding night, Teddy showed no tenderness to his virgin wife. As a matter of fact, he was so aggressive that she insisted on separate bedrooms afterward. By the early twentieth century, Teddy's emotional instability had become full-blown depression—putting even more strain on the relationship. They divorced in 1913.

In 1908, while still technically, though not emotionally, married and in her mid-forties, Edith met and fell for a journalist named Morton Fullerton. For Wharton, this was unequivocal love. She savored sex for the first time in her life. Alas, for the dashing and promiscuous Fullerton, it was but one of many liaisons he was involved in. We have the letters to prove it. In *The Book of Love: Writers and Their Love Letters*, Cathy N. Davidson writes, "The affair between Wharton and Fullerton lasted several years but with different degrees of intensity and commitment for each lover. To a modern reader perusing the Wharton half of this correspondence, it is obvious that the passion of her life was a dalliance in his."

The first time I read that sentence I felt uneasy because I saw my experience reflected clearly in the words, "the passion of her life was a dalliance in his." How unfortunate to be the passionate one, I thought. After a while I took comfort in the fact that I wasn't the first woman this has ever happened to. Looking at it now, I see that Wharton's passion was powerful in its own right. In any relationship—even a mutual one—the only set of feelings you can account for are your own. You cannot control or even know exactly what your partner feels. You can trust that he feels the same and openly communicate about how you feel, but the only set of feelings you can sign on the dotted line for are your own. Unrequited love is a chance to practice taking hold of your half—allowing yourself to feel it fully and let it be something special all by itself. Celebrate the fact that you have such a mighty force within you. No, you aren't going to share the passion with him but you will keep it for yourself and let it take on a new, as yet unseen, form. It was a passion in her life. End of sentence.

Now, who is Morton Fullerton? I have no idea. Edith Wharton, on the other hand, she was the first woman to win a Pulitzer Prize—for her novel *The Age of Innocence* in 1921. Looks like she found a place to put that passion. On Fullerton's Wikipedia page it says, "Known For: His affair with award-winning author, Edith Wharton and work with the *London Times*." Well it's a good thing she took a liking to you, isn't it, Fulley? Otherwise history might have lost your phone number. I believe he saw her as a vehicle to immortally, or maybe just money, while he was alive. Wharton asked him to destroy all the letters she had written him. He didn't.

A few years ago I was involved with a man and when we stopped seeing each other I worried about what it meant to him. Will he remember me the way I remember him? Did I make a lasting impression on him the way he did on me? At some point I thought about that little sentence describing one woman's passion vs. a man's dalliance and seeing how well her passion served her in other ways, and I chose not to care. I don't

care what he did or didn't feel. What he does or doesn't remember. I am a person and I count. It meant something to me,
therefore it meant something. I will now take my passion and
do what I damn well please. How extraordinary to be the passionate one.

THREE

SILENCE YOUR INNER PSYCHO

When you're a beautiful person on the inside, nothing in the world can change that about you. Jealousy is the result of one's lack of self-confidence, self-worth, and self-acceptance. The Lesson: If you can't accept yourself, then certainly no one else will.

—Sasha Azevedo

Each of us is one sudden action away from being put in a straightjacket. All it takes is your conscience to go on a quick bathroom break, leaving one of those crazy little thoughts unattended, and boom—back-to-back life sentences. What if you really did sprinkle arsenic into your boss's iced Americano or strolled over to your ex's house to meet his wife and show her your shiny new pickaxe?

Fortunately, for most of us, these are just passing thoughts—dismissed with a shake of the head and a deep sigh. There is, however, a special subset of madness that pops up when we're under the influence of jealousy, envy, and obsession—emotions synonymous with unrequited love (and sometimes requited love). Some of the behaviors that accompany these emotions—such as incessant cyberstalking; driving by his house just to see if his car is there; bringing him up in every conversation you have, regardless of how well you know the person you're talking to—are not exactly illegal but not entirely sane either.

When this behavior feels necessary, it means your ego has taken over. The inmate is running the asylum. The ego is the voice in your head that says "should" a lot. He *should* be with me and not her. I *should* have been married years ago. I *should* teach him a lesson. I *should* have control over this situation. The shoulds can keep us from enjoying, or even noticing, what *is*—i.e., reality. Sometimes the sound of should is so strong in our minds that we try to inflict it on others. The frustration mounts when we can't make people see or feel what we think they should, and the only person we end up hurting in the grand attempt to do so is me, myself, and I.

The antidote to the ego is the voice of your true self. This voice says, "I am" a lot. I am compassionate. I am hopeful. I am capable of love. I am hurt. I am disappointed things didn't work out. This entity accepts what is and works from there. It recognizes that what it is feeling—what *you* are feeling—is for you to process. If the ego feels bad, it's going to try and take everyone else down with it. This is when we start to look a little unstable from the outside. Most people forgive us to a certain extent because, hey, they've been there, too. By projecting pain outward, however, rather than processing it inward, it lasts longer. I know certain ego-inspired actions feel really good; as with any drug, you experience euphoria at first. But the ultimate consequences are harmful.

DON'T STALK (OR CYBERSTALK)

Most likely, everyone has been guilty of cyberstalking at one time or another, which either makes us completely normal or collectively insane. Or we could go with collectively curious. As with everything, however, curiosity can get out of hand. I've cyber-spied on men I've dated, as well as the women in their lives. I once called a guy's work phone (after business hours, of course) just to hear the sound of his voice, and I've done the drive by. It was really sweet, actually. I was with a good girl-friend, and with my hand covering my eyes I made my pathetic request: "Can we drive by his house?" She didn't ask any questions, she just drove. His car was there, which I found intriguing, although I can't remember what I did with this classified piece of information. I do know, however, that it gave me a sense of control—a false one; that's always the case when you look in on someone's life, whether real or virtual. *Ah ha! I know where he is.* As if the knowing could somehow stop him from shuffling over to his girlfriend's house later. Another result of peeking in on someone's life is that it makes us feel sorry for ourselves, which, let's be honest, is sometimes pleasurable. *Why not sit here and look at photos of his pretty girlfriend? I do so prefer that to snapping out of it and living my own life.*

It's natural to wonder what he's up to, but it's most healthy to do so every four to six months, maybe every year, ideally every few years. Obsession is when we wonder about him every other day (and justify it by calling it "curiosity"). If you're constantly looking in on someone you've never dated, either hoping today is the day or suffering by comparing yourself to his woman, you are absorbed by a mirage. You're stuck in neutral, mired in a fantasy, while life is passing you by. Take a moment. Step outside the daydream. Find out what's happening in the "real world." Meet new people. Harboring this obsession keeps you distracted from potential mates. You may think, Won't I just meet someone new when the time comes? It may take longer if you're busy comparing every guy to the one you're cyberstalking. Clean out your mental closet. A clear head will leave you better prepared for meeting someone new. If it's your ex and/or his new lady friend that you're constantly checking in on, then you're picking at a scab. It's going to take that much longer to heal.

It took one photo to stop me from sticking my hand in the boiling pot of cyberstalking: an engagement photo. I had unfriended this guy months before, but I found out he was engaged and went poking around. The photo wasn't of the two of them; it was a close-up of her hand holding a glass of champagne—diamond radiating, of course. Afterward I wondered why I hadn't just stuck a pencil in my eye instead; it would have been more pleasant. When you realize all you're doing by visiting someone's profile page is hurting yourself, it's time to step up the self-love and stop. There is an iron door between me and this man's Facebook page now. I figure his photos probably don't look all that different than those of any other couple (or person) playing the social media game of "Look How Great My Life Is," so I have an idea of what's going on without actively dipping my toe in the molten lava.

Dialing back the cyberstalking is a good exercise for your overall self-discipline. Nothing substantial gets done without self-discipline—not swimming the English Channel, starting your own clothing line, or loving one person for the rest of your life. Think of it this way: if you can't control your social media usage now, you won't be able to control it when you're in a relationship, either. Social media habits are a big point of contention for couples. Let us not forget, relationships don't change you. *You* change you. Facebook is a fine thing—it's how we keep in touch and good can come from it. Just take a break every now and then to make sure you have more control over it than it has over you. Maybe pick one day a week that you dedicate entirely to the flesh-and-blood relationships in your life.

When curiosity does get the better of us and we do check-in on a stud or two, it's important to remember what we're looking at isn't real. In a January 2013 article for *The Frisky* called "The Case Against Cyberstalking Your Ex's New Love," Ami Angelowicz writes, "But I've come to understand that social media is like a funhouse. It warps everything, makes it giant or small or headless, unrecognizable, most notably your sense of self and reality. It takes your imagination on a wild tilt-a-whirl of imagined scenarios and possibilities. It's a warped mirror reflecting your worst fears and deepest insecurities." Social media is a cocktail party. Everyone is dressed up—makeup and couture covering all the flaws. We still don't know what really goes on at home.

CEASE AND DESIST DISCUSSING YOUR SORROW WITH *EVERYONE*

In a nook off the West Balcony of Grand Central Station is a cocktail lounge called The Campbell Apartment. Once the opulent office of 1920s business tycoon John W. Campbell (no affinity to Campbell's Soup), it's an inspired space reminiscent of old, glamorous New York. I worked there as a hostess for a year and, in the early days of my job, loved stepping back in time with every shift. After a few months there, I experienced what I'll call The Great Heartbreak of 2003. Suddenly the lounge—designed to resemble a thirteenth-century Florentine palazzo—did nothing for me. This was the first time an inward despair colored everything on my outside world completely and unmistakably gray.

I was at Campbell one night sharing hostess duties with a girl named Rhonda, who had always been friendly. There was a lull in the evening and I realized Rhonda and I had six more hours together to go—surely I could profess my misery to her. She indulged me at first and had some sensible things to say, but I wanted more. The more I talked about my heartbreak the more I wanted her to tell me how to fix it. I was growing restless and she was, understandably, annoyed. I could see her irritation and I couldn't stop. Eventually I went on break and promised myself no more assaulting Rhonda. Looking back, I'm mortified by my behavior.

When a promising relationship goes awry, we inadvertently become bleeding-heart narcissists. It's suddenly a struggle to change the subject away from thyself. This is understandable when the wound is fresh. You've been blindsided, and your friends will rush to your aide. They will Skype all night, rock you to sleep, or refresh your ice cream bowl and shot glass as many times as you need. But after the initial shock passes—the first two weeks, maybe the first month depending on how long the relationship lasted—you must limit the number of people you discuss it with. Pick two or three individuals—your nearest and dearest—to keep confiding in, but remember you have to be careful even with them. They want to help you, but they have troubles of their own and they're not mental health professionals. Even if they are, they're off duty. Their desire to help you may clash with their seeming inability to.

The quest to mention your misery at every opportunity—as was my case with Rhonda—is in fact a desperate search to find the one person who is going to tell you exactly what you want to hear. *Surely someone around here has the antidote to Love Potion No. 9.* But consider that no one can advise you when your heart is broken, because there's really only one thing you want to hear: "It's not over! He's on his way to your place to patch things up right now." Anything other than that is irritating—especially "Everything's going to be fine. This will make you stronger." While that's true, there's still a depressing, cross-country car ride between here and there.

The next time you want to discuss a broken relationship with friends, ask yourself, "Do I want advice or do I just want to talk?" If you want to talk, then preface the conversation with, "I just need someone to listen." Your friends might breathe a sigh of relief at not having to play Dear Abby. If you ask for advice, you need to be willing to hear what they say without getting defensive—even if they offer tough love. For the most part, what they say—it could be a callous, "Get over it!"—is meant to help you. You may not find it helpful, but you did ask for it. If you regret asking, say so rather than arguing about your pain, "I know I asked, but I'm not ready to hear this."

I advise against discussing the situation with people who live on the periphery of your life. This scenario came to life when my sister once offered to give a guy friend of mine a ride

to the airport. They know each other but aren't close in any
capacity. During the seven-minute drive, he told her that he
was flying to Arizona and his ex-fiancée was there and she still
had his ring. How could he get it back? Should he let her know
he's flying there or not? My sister came home and said, "Dylan
needs to get a grip." Coworkers are a tough call because some
double as friends. If you spend time with your coworkers outside the office, then share away. Rhonda and I were not friends
away from the hostess stand, and I should not have assumed
her shoulder was there for my leaning.

Being able to put the brakes on when talking about your
despair is not just for others' sake but also your own. By discussing, overanalyzing, and evoking every single memory,
you're dwelling on the pain. You're getting comfy in the corner
of feeling sorry for yourself. At first your heart was legitimately
broken, but you can start running a Woe Is Me campaign
without realizing it. Eckhart Tolle explains how we get to this
place: "As long as part of your sense of self is invested in your
emotional pain, you will unconsciously resist or sabotage every
attempt that you make to heal the pain. Why? Quite simply
because you want to keep yourself intact, and the pain has become an essential part of you. This is an unconscious process,
and the only way to overcome it is to make it conscious."

Disciplining yourself into not discussing your troubles every
chance you get is one way to make the process conscious. It will
be difficult—you will nod your way through conversations
when all you want to do is talk about you—but as you feel the
desire to talk about your pain rise within you, also feel yourself
say no. Do the same with social media. Look at the little devil
on your shoulder telling you to cyber-check your ex and flick

the fucker away. In doing so, you're choosing to take back your life.

BUT WHO'S GOING TO MAKE HIM FEEL BAD?!

One factor that can keep us lingering in a man's life longer than necessary is the wanton desire to teach him a lesson. The thinking goes, "Oh I would walk away, but he can't treat people like this. He certainly can't treat ME like this. Someone has to show him."

What I've learned the hard way is you can't force someone feel the way you want them to. You may want him to feel guilty, remorseful about how he treated you. You may want him to feel as bad as he made you feel. But take it from me: it's not possible. You can take a Louisville Slugger to both of his headlights (and with sufficient evidence he can press charges), but that won't make him rethink the way he treated you. It will piss him off. He will call you crazy and he might even re-aim his anger in your direction. Then it becomes a volley of revenge—each of you feeling completely justified in your behavior—but he's still not feeling any contrition. It's entirely possible that at some point he'll feel bad about the way he treated you, but he will do so in his own time.

When I was a sophomore in college I was sleeping with a guy, Archie, who had a girlfriend, Betty. Naturally, I was unhappy about the existence of said girlfriend. It's hard to feel sorry for me, though, I know. I'm not asking for sympathy. I was nineteen years old and wholeheartedly believed I was doing what I needed to do to get him to be with me exclusively. It was also a bit of a power trip. After each sex session he'd get mad and say, "This is never happening again." But it always happened again. He appeared to have no control. I felt quite irresistible.

Eventually Archie and Betty broke up, but it wasn't because of his infidelity; she had no knowledge of that. I'm not sure what happened, but they were through. I didn't rejoice, as it was past the point of my interest; I'd fallen hard for another fraternity boy. I was, nonetheless, perturbed when Archie told me over Christmas break that he and Betty had reconnected, were working things out, and were going to start over in the New Year. I thought about it for a minute, and said, "No." Even though I no longer wanted to be with Archie, I remembered how much he'd hurt me by always going back to Betty, and I wanted him to feel the same pain. I couldn't inflict that pain on him, though, because he didn't feel for me the way he felt for Betty. The only logical thing for me to do, I reasoned, was to make it so he couldn't have Betty. "If you try to get back together with her," I said, "I'll tell her you've been sleeping with me this whole time." He begged me not to, but the cement had solidified around my decision.

Knowing he had little choice, he told her himself. She was crushed but not for long. I imagine he got down on his knees immediately and swore to be a new-and-improved boyfriend. She took him back.

I did not like this new development at all. Fortunately, I had another piece of damning information. He had also slept with—just once—a good friend of Betty's, Veronica. This time I didn't bother to give him a heads up that I was going to let Betty know, I just did—by way of telling her roommate.

Guess who got blamed for the whole thing? This girl right here. It was all my fault. Archie said I ruined his life. Betty said I ruined her life. I have no idea if Veronica was held accountable. I was not an innocent bystander by any means, but I was also not the one being unfaithful. I take that back—I was cheating myself—but that wouldn't have occurred to me at the time. The two of them stayed together. My plan backfired and my ego was crushed under its own weight. I was out of revenge tactics, so there was nothing left to do but feel the pain of the whole situation.

Most love lessons I've had to experience half a dozen times before I finally got it. Not this one. I understood two things immediately: 1. It hurts less to blame the mistress than the man; therefore the mistress is the designated scapegoat and 2. You can't make arrangements for someone to feel a certain way. You can't make him feel love or remorse. I tried to make Archie feel both. People see what they want to see; I certainly saw what I wanted: I looked at Betty and thought, "Why doesn't she get away from him?!" Rather than—oh, I don't know—peering in the mirror and asking myself the same thing. I looked at Archie asked, "Why is he treating me this way?" instead of, "Why am I allowing myself to be treated this way?"

Years later, I was living in Manhattan and Archie was passing through town. He asked if he could see me. Within the first hour, he offered an unexpected avalanche of apologies. He went through every incident and apologized. It got to the point where I resisted. "You're sorry. I get it," I said. Looking back, I was too dismissive. Sometimes it takes as much grace to accept an apology as it does to offer one. Archie also asked me if I would consider dating him. Without hesitation I said, "No." It didn't feel triumphant; I was more annoyed than anything else. I thought, Really, you want to date me now. That's such a cliché. Years after that—circa summer 2012—Archie and I met up again. He told me he's happy in an open marriage and invited me to spend a night with him. I respectfully declined. Although, I am glad he found someone who shares his sexual taste.

The best way to let a guy know he cannot treat you badly is to walk away. Don't look back. Walking away doesn't make you a doormat—standing there and continuing to put yourself in his path does. Focus on your life and don't waste energy figuring out how to teach him a lesson. Let life do that for you. At some point his behavior might tap him on the shoulder and say, "You have to face me now." Know, however, that he can still choose not to face it. Serial killer Ted Bundy once said, "I don't feel guilty for anything. I feel sorry for people who feel guilt." There you have it—not everyone experiences remorse. Whether or not he feels bad can't be your concern, though; concentrate on your own healing. By the time this apology came my way I didn't need it anymore. I am grateful Archie extended it, but I would have gone on my merry way regardless.

My behavior has caught up with me, too. I look back on certain situations and recoil at the decisions I made. In some cases I've reached out and apologized. In others, like this one, I've reconciled my behavior within and recognize that in failing to honor or respect others, I dishonor myself, above all.

Everything that irritates us about others can lead us to an understanding of ourselves.

—Carl Jung

HOT COGNITION VS. COLD COGNITION

You're most likely familiar with hot and cold cognition; you just don't know it yet. Let's say you're in your house and you know you're going to see your ex at a party later in the evening. Your mind is clear and your cognition is cold. You say to yourself, *I'm not going to sleep with him,* and you mean it. It happened once before, you were hurt and you want to avoid going to that dismal place again. It's more than reasonable.

At the party you somehow end up in a dimly lit corner with Valentino, and the flickering candlelight accentuates those dimples you do so adore. He leans in for a sweet, harmless kiss. Uh oh—those sensible thoughts you had earlier are now being covered up by lust, spreading itself out like smooth peanut butter all over your cerebral cortex. Your cognition has swiftly gone from cold to hot, and—yikes—your loins are on fire. Wine or no wine, you are under the influence, and saying no is no longer an option.

Hot cognition essentially means one emotion takes over your brain and your choices are influenced entirely by that emotion. Lust isn't the only emotion that makes for low-quality decision making; anger is another, as is jealousy. Anger/Hot Cognition, Exhibit A: Any professional or college basketball coach during a botched play. After a bout of anger has ended and cognition turns cold again, we often have to backtrack and apologize publicly or privately: "I said some things I didn't mean." Keep in mind that other people's cognition gets hot, too, and you might be a factor in their irrational decisions. Consider my situation with Archie, previously mentioned: I was right that he couldn't control his desire but not because he had feelings for me; rather, it was because the heating system in his frontal lobe was functioning properly. Pay attention to the way a guy treats you when his cognition is cold. Archie's cognition cooled quickly, and that's when he would announce "this is never happening again."

Psychologist and political scientist Robert Paul Abelson made the distinction between hot and cold cognition in 1963. Unfortunately, five decades later, we are still held accountable for all decisions we make, hot cognition notwithstanding. Knowing about this mental shift, however, can be helpful. Consider putting some precautions in place when your cognition is cold to keep yourself in check when it suddenly turns hot. For example, avoid hanging out in dark corners with men you know it's best not to sleep with. Maybe even avoid being alone with them altogether. If you feel yourself getting angry with a friend because she's telling you to get over a guy, end the conversation. Change the subject if you can, or call her back later if you can't calm down. If you see that some cute girl left a flirtatious comment on your crush's Facebook page and jealousy flares up, back away from your computer and turn off your phone. Put your sneakers on and go for a run. Run furiously. Take it all out on the pavement—no one can take a screenshot of that.

JEALOUSY, ENVY & EVOLUTION

And the award for the Emotion That Incites the Most Creative Types of Temporary Insanity goes to . . . jealousy. In all seriousness, jealousy is no joke. People feel completely justified killing based on this passion. It's often cited as evidence of love.

Would I get so upset if I didn't love you so much? Erich Fromm counters, "Envy, jealousy, ambition, any kind of greed are passions; love is an action, the practice of human power, which can be practiced only in freedom and never as the result of a compulsion."

Jealousy is an incredibly telling emotion; if you listen to what it's saying to you—rather than hold other people accountable for it—you will pull back the curtain further on who you are and what you want. An article in the August 2009 issue of *Psychology Today* called "Love's Destroyer" proclaims jealousy the wayward guardian of relationships; it's the fear of being replaced by another person. This obviously rings true of romantic unions, but it could be any relationship. There's sibling rivalry, office competition, and platonic jealousy. Jealousy can ignite the famous fury that hell hath not.

Jealousy comes from treating another person like a possession, so part of overcoming it is accepting that you do not own anyone. You might not mean to think of someone else as an object, but jealousy indicates you subconsciously do. In moderation, jealousy can be a good thing. If you see your man talking to a pretty girl at a party and it makes you appreciate what you have, then take it. If you go home and slam the door in his face, there's a problem. In romantic relationships and friendships you are there because you choose to be and the other person chooses to be; at any point one party can opt to go elsewhere. This is the risk of all human relationships. Jealousy is the fear that the person is about to be taken away and panic ensues. But another person cannot be taken away; he can only choose to go. Therefore jealousy is a lack of respect for the other person's free will. You are trying to control him—keep him there—rather than trust his ability to choose or your ability to survive if he does go.

In the same *Psychology Today* article, Marcianne Blévis, a psychiatrist and psychoanalyst practicing in Paris, told the magazine, "All human emotions exist to help us figure out who we are in the world, and jealousy is no exception. It is a resource we call on when we feel at risk, when our sense of self is put in jeopardy. When we are jealous, we are in fact in the grip of an identity crisis." She recommends, "not to blame one's partner for attention to someone else, which is what we usually do, but to look inside oneself." Inside is where, Blevis believes, "we will find the source of insecurity that instantly makes the rival seem so superior."

Although the words are often used interchangeably, jealousy is different from envy. According to *Psychology Today*, "'Jealousy arises when a relationship is infringed on by a rival who threatens to take away something that is in a sense rightfully yours,'" explains Richard Smith, professor of psychology at the University of Kentucky. "Envy, on the other hand, derives from the basic fact that so much of the spoils of life come from how we compare to others. It arises when another person possesses some trait or object that you want, and includes a mix of discontent, a sense of inferiority, and a frustration that may be tinged with resentment." Envy is more sorrow-based than jealousy; specifically, it often inspires us to feel sorry for ourselves: *I'm so lame. I'll never be like* [insert object of envy here]. You can envy the fact that a woman is married (without having any attraction to her husband); you can also covet her shoe collection, well-paying job, or waist size.

The occasional twinge of wanting what someone else has (or appears to have) is normal, but when you actively don't like a person because he or she has something you want or when you're blaming that person for the way you feel, it's emotionally counterproductive. Try this instead: First, admit to yourself that you're envious. You don't have to admit it to anyone else, and you don't have to do anything about it—yet. I find that sometimes envy dissipates upon admission. If it doesn't dissolve, dig deeper. Identify what it is she has that you want. Suppose she has her own business. Do you really want your own business? *No, actually, I don't feel I have any business acumen but she has a thing to call her own and I want the same.* Then take action. Search for that thing you can call your own: take painting classes; join the running club; or volunteer at the local food bank. Do something for you that you've always wanted to do, or try something completely new on a whim.

If you envy someone because of beauty or money then all you need do is look at celebrity relationships for evidence that these two elements do not in any way guarantee lasting love, an extended career, or infinite happiness. If you envy someone (everyone) because they are in a relationship—and are seemingly in love—then remember that no love exists without self-love, and if you're longing for someone else's life you aren't loving yourself. I know it's aggravating to keep being told everything comes back to you. It really is easier to blame others. Once you get used to asking yourself what's going on, however, you realize you have so much more control over your life than you originally thought. You are no longer subject to other people's mood swings and opinions.

Whether you're experiencing envy or jealousy depends on the specific unrequited situation. If you're on the outside look-ing in, it's usually envy, but we can certainly be found guilty of claiming other people as our possessions. I was on break at the Campbell Apartment one night, and I sat at the lower-level bar where Jake the bartender gave me a well-disguised shot of Bailey's. A group of girls were visiting him and one of them walked over and introduced herself. She said, "Hi I'm Carly, Jake's girlfriend." When she left I told Jake how she'd intro-duced herself, and he was highly irritated. She was declaring him as her own and he would not be possessed.

By my early thirties I'd hoped I was done with jealousy, but it snuck up on me one winter day. Do you remember James T. Kirk? The Star Fleet captain who was in my class? Asked me out. Blew me off. Yeah, him. Well, there was a third party involved—another girl in our class, who also happened to be a new friend of mine. Sometimes I wondered if there was some-thing going on between the two; during certain weeks, it seemed maybe yes, while during others, definitely no. The three of us had met at the exact same time. No one had dibs on anyone else, so I didn't mention it to her. I thought bringing it up it would make it seem as if I were telling her to stay away from him, which was not my place to do. All I had was a crush.

Once he asked me out, however, I became hypersensitive to what was happening around me. After the lecture one day, she walked up to him and I could hear the two of them making plans. Jealousy rose in me like an infuriated tide. It felt as though a hand reached out of my stomach and grabbed me by the throat. I thought it best to leave the room. It had been a long time since I'd felt full-on hot cognition jealousy. This was the first time, however, that I recognized it as an evolutionary reaction. There was no logic here. There was about to be a showdown—not between her and me but between my biological makeup and me.

ME: Can I help you?

BIO: Go back in there. She's taking him away from you.

ME: First of all, he's not mine to take. More important, she's been nothing but nice to me.

BIO: Trickery! If she took him away from you in the wilderness, she'd be taking away your hunter. You're going to starve.

ME: We're not in the fucking wilderness. There's a 7-Eleven right there.

BIO: You can't reproduce with her.

ME: Re-pro-duce? You really think offspring fit into our budget right now?

BIO: It's your primary function!

ME: Ugh, you haven't even made it to the Stone Age yet.

BIO: He's the Alpha male.

ME: That'll happen when there are only four heterosexual men in one class.

BIO: Still. He has much to offer you.

ME: Offer me. What has he given me? Huh? This semester what has he given me? Nothing. She, on the other hand, has given me Sun Chips and Tylenol. She let me sip her Arizona Iced Tea. She gave me a ride home that one time. She is much more conducive to my survival in graduate school than he is.

BIO: Think. Think real hard about what he can give you that she can't. I'll give you a hint: it's more satisfying than Sun Chips.

ME: Yeah, well, he withdrew his invitation for Sun Chips by candlelight, didn't he?

BIO: That's obviously her fault!

ME: Will you and your warped perception please leave me alone?

BIO: Has it escaped your attention that we're in heat?!

ME: As if you'd let me forget for more than forty-five minutes.

BIO: I *need* to go to Pound Town.

ME: Did you seriously just say that?

BIO: Yes! [*sticks fingers in ears*] Coitus! Coitus! Coitus! Coitus! Coitus! Coitus!

ME: That's very mature.

BIO: Coitus! Coitus! Coitus! Coitus! Coitus! Coitus!

ME: [*hits forehead head against wall*] Is that all you ever think about?

BIO: I think about food sometimes.

I didn't say anything to her until the last day of the semester when there were six weeks of not seeing him ahead. She and I went to brunch and I brought it up. My perception at this point was that she was interested in him and he was blowing her off, too. I was wrong. She spoke casually, "Oh yeah. He took me out to lunch and I hung out at his place one night right around Hurricane Sandy,* but nothing happened. I wasn't feeling flir-

* Same time he asked me out

tatious. I mean, we're friends." Real-Life Assessment: I was interested in him. He was interested in her. She was suffering over some guy who sent her scathing e-mails. And so it goes. This was hard for me to hear, actually, because he really could have skipped asking me out altogether, but again, his doing, not hers.

She then made an interesting comment, "I wish you would have told me. I would have gotten out of your way." I responded assuredly, "In that case I'm glad I didn't tell you. I don't want him hanging out with me just because you're unavailable." It felt good to say. There once was a time when I would've kicked myself for not bringing it up and thereby missing out on his secondhand company. Those days are gone.

The one relationship that did work out is she and I. We're thick as thieves. This friendship could easily have gotten mangled based on a false claim of ownership or misperception. While my biology has some catching up to do, my emotional evolution felt right on track.

> *Jealousy is a disease, love is a healthy condition. The immature mind often mistakes one for the other, or assumes that the greater the love, the greater the jealousy—in fact, they are almost incompatible; one emotion hardly leaves room for the other.*
>
> —Robert A. Heinlein, *Stranger in a Strange Land*

I ONLY HEAR WHAT I WANT TO

In 1974 Maya Angelou (b. 1928) followed up her critically acclaimed *I Know Why the Caged Bird Sings* with another compelling memoir entitled *Gather Together in My Name*. The

book opens with Maya at the age of seventeen living in post–
World War II San Francisco. She was working as a cook at
The Creole Café when "God's prettiest man became a cus-
tomer at my restaurant." He was thirty-one and his nickname
was Curly. They quickly became a couple and he showed her a
brand of affection she had never known.

Early on, Curly confessed that he was engaged and as
soon as he received word that his fiancée's job in a shipyard
was finished, they would go to New Orleans and get married.
Maya confessed, "I hastily stored the information in that in-
accessible region of the mind where one puts the memory of
pain and other un-pleasantries. For the while it needn't
bother me, and it didn't." She continued to enjoy her days
enamored with him. "At playland on the beach we rode the
Ferris wheel and the loop-the-loop and gooed ourselves with
salt-water taffy . . . then went to his hotel and one more, or
two more, or three more love parties. I never wanted it to
end."

True to his word, two months after they met, Curly announced it was time to go. He told Maya that she would make
a wonderful wife someday and left. She was inundated with
sorrow. She knew the entire time he planned to leave and she
disregarded it. She wrote, "Because he had not lied, I was for-
bidden anger. Because he had patiently and tenderly taught me
love, I could not use hate to ease the pain. I had to bear it." Her
grief was palpable. She concluded that every sad song on the
radio had been written for her. She lost weight. She wrote,
"The loss of young first love is so painful that it borders on the
ludicrous."

Consider when falling for someone that he is telling you everything you need to know and, in some cases, you choose to look straight ahead in the other direction. Selective hearing is a dangerous side effect of sudden onset *amour*. This situation is extreme; not many men pursuing a woman say upfront that they're getting married, but it's not entirely unheard of. Let it be known that I'm not criticizing Maya. First of all, she's my hero. Second of all, she was seventeen years old. Above all, she describes the scenario so beautifully and accurately that I'm glad she experienced it for that reason alone. I'm using her story to illustrate how easy it is to ignore facts that are staring us in the face.

In fairness, the first time anyone is fully immersed in infatuation, it's usually the same story: It lifts you up (really high), then lets you down (really low), and no one can convince you to see reason in the interim. Because infatuation feels fresh every time, even in your second or third run-in you may find yourself saying, No, THIS time it's real. This ONE is perfect. I ignored warning signs before but now I KNOW I have it right. After the third or thirteenth time, it's a good idea to take some precautions.

The first precaution is simple. Tell yourself you're infatuated. Bring some awareness into what's happening. It's pleasurable, yes, but it's an artificial feeling that isn't going to last forever. Just know that you're in the zone. You've had a few too many wine coolers and now you're going to drink a little water. Present-moment thinking can help. One might say Maya was living in the present by ignoring Curly's future marriage. But no—in that present moment, the man was engaged. She may've thought she could change that inconvenient fact, as many of us do. *Engaged? Surely he'll break it off with her and be with me.* That's the euphoria talking. Tell it to take a cold shower.

A man's attachment to another isn't the only thing we think we can change. There are also bad habits: anger management issues, promiscuity, or drinking habits; we predict they will magically evaporate just because we want them to. It's partially the fault of fairytales, I suppose, where frogs turn into princes and angry beasts turn into genial gentlemen. When dating someone, ask yourself if you can live with his flaws—step out of character and assume it will not change. Snoring: annoying, yes, deal breaker, no. Getting so drunk he calls me vicious names and swears he doesn't remember the next morning: survey says, hell no.

Eckhart Tolle recommends looking to the past and the future for practical purposes only. Practically looking to future means having a 401(k) and an umbrella, and practically looking to the past means learning from your mistakes. Maya Angelou might say, "When I was seventeen, I dated a man who was engaged and ended up devastated, do I want to do that again?" Someone else might say "Last time I was obsessed with a guy, I blew off all my friends because I thought I didn't need them anymore. I probably don't want to repeat that."

Pay attention not only to his present behavior but also yours. "I'm spending money that I don't have" or "I'm sitting in a restaurant by myself—he's late again." Try to infuse a little reason into the madness. I know that sounds like sacrilege. Perhaps you're saying, "You can't infuse reason into love!" But if you don't try to sprinkle some good sense on the situation now, you'll hit the stone-cold floor of reality later, like Maya did (again, not criticizing—just using the example). It's not fair to him, or to you, to pretend he's perfect. Get to know him— flaws and all—and be honest with yourself about what is and isn't acceptable.

FOUR

LOVE VS. ADDICTION

But I still love to wash in your old bath water
Love to think that you couldn't love another
I can't help it . . . you're my kind of man
—From the song "Bathwater," lyrics by No Doubt

In the last chapter we talked about trying to get a handle on some of our broken-heart-inspired impulses. The first essential step is to want to stop an obsession and all its accompanying behavior. Nothing will change until you admit to yourself that you're obsessed and that you're ready for the mania to end. You may be fixated on one person or possessed by an idea: "Marriage, marriage, marriage. White picket fence. Fence. Fence." What enabled me to break out of this cycle of dysfunction was not just knowing but understanding how much I was hurting myself in the process. It took a while for me to fully realize this. There were several instances of, How did I end up here again? Oh right, I did the exact same thing I've done dozens of times before. Only when we *want* to stop can we put forth the authentic effort to do so. Afterward we end up wondering, Why didn't I do this sooner? It doesn't matter. We're doing it now. In cases where we refuse to stop or we casually convince ourselves that we can stop whenever we want (but then don't), there may be a more serious issue. Perhaps just beneath the surface we're afraid we're *unable* to call the whole thing off.

There are two types of addiction: substance addiction and process addiction. Most of us are familiar with substance addiction—the uncontrollable need to use alcohol and/or legal or illegal drugs. A process addiction, also referred to as a behavioral addiction, is the compulsion to engage in a behavior that can otherwise be considered normal. For example, one can be addicted to food, sex, Internet use, or another person. It's easy for addicts to dismiss process addictions because they are a part of everyday life for others. "Everybody needs to eat," they say. "What's wrong with a little porn now and again?" "I don't check Facebook *that* much." "God, I'm *not* obsessed with him!" It's also easy for non-addicts to reject that process addiction actually exists because, "You *should be able* to control yourself." Make no mistake; a process addiction can be just as devastating—to the addict and the people in his or her life—as a substance addiction.

We know that chemical changes take place in the brain when falling in love, which puts us at risk for becoming addicted to the process. The Love Addicts Anonymous (LAA) website (loveaddicts.org) explains, "Love addiction comes in many forms. Some love addicts carry a torch for unavailable people. Some love addicts obsess when they fall in love. Some love addicts get addicted to the euphoric effects of romance. Others cannot let go of a toxic relationship even if they are unhappy, depressed, lonely, neglected or in danger." It took me .3 seconds to identify myself on the list: Torchbearer. Here's the LAA definition: "Torchbearers obsess about someone who is unavailable. This can be done without acting out (suffering in silence) or by pursuing the person they are in love with. Some Torchbearers are more addicted than others. This kind of addiction feeds on fantasies and illusions. It is also known as unrequited love." Sound familiar? If it doesn't, there are many other types of love addiction listed on the website.

Some are skeptical about the idea of addiction being associated with love. When I told a friend about LAA she said, "Aren't all women love addicts?" No, actually, some are in healthy relationships or single and thriving. Clinical addiction aside, we can all agree there are unhealthy behaviors and patterns that can be part of the pursuit of love. If you can't fully embrace the idea of love as a process addiction, consider LAA as a place that lists some of the most common unhealthy behaviors associated with relationships.

I was surprised to see so many love-related maladies listed on the LAA website; although, each one does make perfect sense (I diagnosed myself, some of my friends, and a few of the guys I've dated—couldn't help it). It emphasized for me further our tendency to use relationships to veil personal problems. According to Eckhart Tolle, "Every addiction starts with pain and ends with pain. Whatever the substance you are addicted to —alcohol, food, legal or illegal drugs, or a person— you are using something or somebody to cover up your pain. That's why after the initial euphoria has passed, there's so much unhappiness, so much pain in intimate relationships. They do not cause pain and unhappiness. They *bring out* the pain and unhappiness that is already in you. Every addiction does that. Every addiction reaches a point where it does not work for you anymore, and then you feel the pain more intensely than ever."

Most of us have an emotional malfunction or two that keeps us from loving to our maximum potential. Your mission, should you choose to accept it, is to search for that shortcoming now rather than forwarding it into the future where you hope a relationship is waiting to absolve you of it. If you get to the heart of your own matter, you will go into all relationships clearheaded and openeyed rather than in I-need-another-hit mode.

LOVE AND LIMERENCE

Throughout my life I've found it difficult to move past romantic feelings for a guy with any speed or ease. Even in seventh grade I remember looking at my classmates floating from one boyfriend to another and wondering how they were switching their feelings so fast. Of course they probably weren't—they were most likely trying to live up to social expectations. Me, I would quietly nurture a crush for years. It never occurred to me not to. My mind was preprogrammed to think, "If at first you don't succeed . . ."

In college this manifested itself in new ways as I navigated the hook-up culture. A casual hook-up for him could mean months of longing and wondering how to win him over for me. Meanwhile there were other guys asking me out, but I was so preoccupied with that one over there that I couldn't be bothered. A few times I chose to date one of the guys who professed interest in me while I still harbored strong feelings for another. My motivation was genuine; I wanted to move on and hoped passion for the man who actually liked me would form, but it never worked out that way.

When I was twenty-four, I ran into a guy I knew my freshman year of college. Remember Jack and Rose from Chapter One? Rose had an unrequited crush and offered to take her shirt off for Jack—him. It was Labor Day weekend 2003 and he looked incredible. He had muttonchops—not just sideburns, full, down-the-face chops. He was so gorgeous that he managed to make muttonchops look appetizing. Who does that? And so it began. On our first date he said, "I had such a crush on you in college." I confessed the same and nostalgia blessed our union. For the first time in my life, a relationship felt mutual. I hadn't realized how un-mutual everything had been before. I was chasing the boy or the boy was chasing me but nothing like this. Everything I gave to Jack—sweet sentiments, small gifts, spontaneous oral sex—came back to me times ten. We dated until early December when he started to back away. Just before Christmas he told me he was getting back together with his ex-girlfriend. Anguish set in. Just as I had never known life to be so wonderful with him, I had never known it to be so painful without him.

There was a constant ache in my body, and I couldn't concentrate on anything. He found his way into every one of my thoughts. All pretty standard for a breakup, except it wouldn't go away. The engine wouldn't turn over. Six months, one year, two years went by and I thought about him every day—to varying degrees, but every day. I dated here and there, but my thinking largely was, "No one else will do." I surrendered to the thought that this must be love—what else would swirl around in my head like brandy in a snifter for so long? I concluded that I was blessed and cursed with a deeper capacity to love than other people, which is why a breakup appeared to hurt me so much more than it hurt them.

I was well aware of the fact that Jack and I had only dated for three months, and this recovery time was beyond irrational. But while one part of my brain recognized that my feelings were out of control, another clearly did not. I considered going to therapy but dismissed the idea, thinking, "I am not walking into someone's office and saying, 'I have a bad case of unrequited love.' The therapist will surely say, 'Sweetheart, we deal with real problems here.'"

Three years after Jack, I met a man who I felt just as passionately for. He was tender and charming and offered occasional evidence of our feelings being mutual when we were together—not so much when we weren't. I won't keep you in suspense; it didn't work out. I was so angry at the universe. I thought, You obviously don't want me to be in a relationship. If that's my fate, fine, but can you at least take the longing away? In time, I regained complete control of all that felt previously uncontrollable—never went to his Facebook page, his number was long out of my phone, it had been months since we were even in touch—but my thoughts continued to overwhelm me like a steady avalanche. And then—remember the guy from Chapter Three with the diamond/champagne photo? Him. I found out he got engaged.

Following that heart attack, and the subsequent ambush of negative thoughts, I swallowed my pride and searched for a therapist. If they laugh, they laugh, I thought, but I have to try something. At my first session I had to fill out a form and the last question was, "What brought you here?" I reluctantly wrote, "A man I wanted to marry is getting married." I feared the therapist would ask me, "Do you believe he wanted to marry you?" and I'd have to confess we were never exclusive. She would surely insist I leave. A short while later I entered the office. The therapist shook my hand and invited me to sit while she skimmed my form. She got to the last question and said wholeheartedly, "Oh, that'll send anyone to therapy." I had come to the right place.

From that moment, I was determined to take a proactive approach to treatment. I was done with the ruminating; I wanted to be peel back my personal layers and, above all, to get over this guy without another guy. That's exactly what she wanted for me too. We were good together; she recommended books and I dutifully read them. I was reading one called *Is It Love or Addiction* by Brenda Schaeffer and came across two gems. First, this book introduced me to my soul mate—Erich "Hot German Sausage" Fromm—and the second was the term "limerence." The book doesn't really say what it is; it merely states, "In either case, the rush of intoxicating feelings experienced during the attraction stage of a romance—a state called limerence—is like a drug that can become a substitute for real intimacy."

It was a weird word and I wanted to know more, so I plugged *limerence* into Google. Lo and behold it has its own Wikipedia page, where it said, "Limerence is an involuntary state of mind which results from a romantic attraction to another person combined with an overwhelming, obsessive need to have one's feelings reciprocated." Yes, I might know exactly how that feels. I continued reading, "The psychologist Dorothy Tennov coined the term 'limerence' in her 1979 book *Love and Limerence: The Experience of Being in Love*." I was born in 1979; perhaps that meant something. Then there was this: "Tennov estimates, based on both questionnaire and interview data, that the average limerent reaction duration, from the moment of initiation until a feeling of neutrality is reached, is approximately three years." I felt like I had just met my long-lost twin sister. Oh my God, it's a thing. It's a thing other people go through. It's a thing this woman studied and wrote a book about. Free at last!

My first thought was, This is me, and my second was, No one is going to believe this is real. It also says on the Wikipedia page, "Limerence can be difficult to understand for those who have never experienced it, and it is thus often dismissed by non-limerents as ridiculous fantasy or a construct of romantic fiction." Sweet. All bases covered. I didn't need the general public to believe me, anyway. I'd happened upon something that accounted for my experience with romance up until that point. I was in a position to study and better understand what I was dealing with. The devil you know is better than the devil you don't.

Tennov perfectly describes in *Love and Limerence* the intrusive thought process I'd experienced: "Just as all roads once led to Rome, when your limerence for someone has crystallized, all events, associations, stimuli, experience return your thoughts to the limerent object (LO) with unnerving consistency. At the moment of awakening after the night's sleep, an image of LO springs into your consciousness. And you find yourself inclined to remain in bed pursuing that image and the fantasies that surround and grow out of it. Your daydreams persist throughout the day and are involuntary. Extreme effort of will to stop them produces only temporary surcease." I read that to a friend and she said, "Doesn't that happen with everyone though?" Yes, after a breakup, those thinking patterns are normal to a point. In the limerent person, however, the thoughts don't subside; as per Tennov, they can last up to three years or more.

My therapist was on board with limerence when I told her about it. She hadn't heard of it previously because it's not yet listed in the Diagnostic and Statistical Manual of Mental Disorders (DSM). Around that time, after several months of seeing each other, she had a suggestion. She asked gently, "What if there was a pill that could help you?" I always thought I'd balk at the suggestion of psychiatric medication, but I was open to it if she thought it might help. My biggest fear was having to tell my story all over again to a psychiatrist (who I'd have to see in order to get a prescription). I'd made it that far, though, and decided to keep going. Once in the psychiatrist's office, I explained, as she listened compassionately, "It's like my brain is a brick wall and every brick is a thought—an idea, memory, aspiration—and the mortar between all the bricks is the man. Whatever man I happen to be obsessed with somehow surrounds every thought." She nodded and said, "Your serotonin levels are low." Oh, is that all?

Serotonin is a neurotransmitter, like dopamine, which effects mood. The psychiatrist prescribed me a common antidepressant called Lexapro, which is meant to boost serotonin. I had never thought of myself as being depressed; obsessed, yes, but not depressed. I later learned that Lexapro is also used to treat Obsessive Compulsive Disorder (OCD), which sounded more like it. At first Lexapro made me supremely tired—without an alarm I could sleep for fourteen hours—but eventually it knocked the wall down. I had the ability to then walk over to the pile of bricks and choose my thoughts instead of feeling like they had been assigned to me.

Dorothy Tennov died in 2007 at the age of seventy-eight, and a gentleman named Albert Wakin, MS, who teaches psychology at Sacred Heart University, took over as the expert on limerence. A few years ago I interviewed him for an article I was writing on the topic for *Marie Claire*. He explained that limerence possesses characteristics of both OCD and addiction but is its own condition. It's characterized as an involuntary obsession with one person. He says limerence can manifest itself whether the feelings are reciprocated or unreciprocated. I am a prime example of what happens when it's not reciprocated—the relationship ends yet thoughts continue beyond a reasonable recovery time. Professor Wakin told me things aren't much better when the feelings are mutual. In a relationship, the person with limerence will incessantly rehearse what to say and do, and it will never be perfect enough to satisfy doubts that the significant other could leave at any moment. A person with limerence will also cut her partner incredible amounts of slack—letting him get away with things that are not generally permitted in a healthy relationship. The last question I asked him was, "Do you have limerence?" He replied, "No, but in all my years of practice my heart goes out to people who have limerence more than anyone else." I told him we were lucky to have him.

Lexapro gave me the power to choose my thoughts, but I have to continually work on choosing the right thoughts— nothing self-critical, no comparing myself to other people, no self-pity, no future tripping, and no wondering "what if." The past is behind me, and the future will unfold in its own time. I am here. Retaining my current frame of mind requires medita- tion, prayer, yoga, journal writing, and lots of reading. I am, as we all are, a work in progress.

I took Lexapro and saw my therapist for a year (unfortu- nately, she moved) and have felt balance in my brain ever since. I'm open to indulging both again should the need arise.

BIRDS OF A FEATHER

In early 2010, a familiar name appeared in my suggested friends on Facebook. It was Zach Morris—an adorable blond guy who lived in my neighborhood when I was an awkward adolescent. Zach was four years older, a lifetime when you're a teenager but a refreshing age difference in adulthood. I extended a friend invite and he wrote back asking, "Do I know you?" consider- ately adding, "No offense." I assured him that none was taken and reminded him that he was in my house once—though it wasn't to see me but rather my babysitter, Kelly Kapowski. That detail jogged his memory and after a few exchanges we decided to get together.

Our first date was cozy. The winter weather was unforgiv- ing, and we retreated to a wine bar to warm ourselves with Syrah. Zach—still adorable but more dirty-blond these days— and I had a lively conversation. Considering that we'd never exchanged more than two sentences prior to this, I wasn't sure that would be the case. Of all the dates to go on, I find it especially intriguing to meet up with someone you have a pleasant memory of but don't really know.

Our second date had a similar feel. We escaped the cold with libations and laughter. He suggested we do it again. We didn't. I invited him to a show a girlfriend of mine was singing in the following week. He politely declined and didn't suggest an alternate date, so I figured that was that. I was disappointed but getting used to the drill. Since no crime had been committed, I didn't feel the need to unfriend him. He simply faded into the background of Facebook.

The following year, in August 2011, my article for *Marie Claire* on limerence was published. I reluctantly posted a link to the piece on Facebook. Normally sharing articles with friends isn't a problem—especially when I'm published in a well-known women's magazine. In this case, however, it was a little different because I had written about something that could be considered pathological. Interestingly, I have no qualms whatsoever with strangers reading about my mental state. The thought of people who know me reading it, however, made me shudder with self-consciousness. Despite my hesitation, I shared the link.

My friends were kind—many of them asking if I was okay. I assured them that all was well and explained there's often lag time between when an article idea is conceived and when it makes it to print. My decision to share had turned out to be a fine one—no harm, no foul. Then I received a private message from Zach. I was surprised to see his name. We

hadn't had any contact—other than status updates—in over a
year. He wrote:

> Hey, I know it has been a long while but I read your article
> about limerence and it really hit home for me. I went
> through this and I'm still going through the exact same
> thing as you. I met this woman a couple of years ago, we hit
> it out of the park and I was on cloud nine with her. I thought
> I had finally met the woman of my dreams; we dated for
> about 6 months with no real problems. It was extremely
> passionate, you know fireworks every time we were to-
> gether. It was like nothing I have ever experienced before.
> At one point I noticed she was distancing herself from me
> and I could tell she just wasn't interested anymore. She
> didn't want a relationship and she didn't want to make a
> future together. So we broke up, which I thought I would
> have no problem doing, but I went into this deep depres-
> sion, I thought about her day and night. I was never happy,
> never. We actually ended up getting back together for like
> two weeks a year after the first break up. So I was feeling
> great for those two weeks but when it ended, I went way
> down this time and I went down bad, it wasn't pretty. Noth-
> ing seemed to help, I drank way too much to try and help
> the pain. Dated a lot of women for no good reason. I blamed
> myself endlessly for screwing the whole relationship. I really
> thought I was such a horrible person that I deserved this. I
> had no one to talk to about what I was going through either,
> everyone just told me to move on and she wasn't worth
> it, but that didn't help. I could only see the good things
> about her.

Well eventually I decided to seek help and found a great therapist and like you, got on Lexapro. Which seemed to help with the obsessive part of me and makes me smile again if just a little. In the end I have learned so much about myself that I would have never known if it wasn't for this breakup. It's kind of a blessing in a way. Not that I would want anyone going through what you and I have gone through, it is the pits. But it does make you stronger in the end. I just thought I'd share cause I feel like the only one sometimes that has ever gone through this. Good luck with your treatment, and I hope you find that happiness.

After this, my decision to share the article was upgraded from fine to brilliant. I was beside myself. It was really thoughtful of him to take the time to write this to me; it's a never-ending comfort to know you're not alone in your experience.

USING THIS ONE TO GET OVER THAT ONE

Let's zoom in on something Zach wrote. In his message he said that he "dated a lot of women for no good reason." Many people use dating as a way to move on from a broken heart, and they end up hurting the person, or people, they temporarily turn to for comfort. There's nothing you can do to stop them from this behavior; you can't even inquire as to whether they're doing it or not. I can't start first dates off with, "So is there any girl in the galaxy that you'd rather be with? 'Cause if there is, I'll leave right now." It's a risk I have to continue taking if I want to meet a long-term match. We can, however, protect ourselves by not taking the rejection personally and accepting that when we stop hearing back from someone, it's not going any further. New Rule: If you don't hear back from a guy or he ends things abruptly, instead of asking, "What's wrong with me?" say, "He did me a favor." Without knowing exactly what the favor is yet, trust that you have been saved a lot of trouble.

Sometimes the favor will come from the fact that the guy is a jerk and you're better off without him. Or maybe he's not a jerk at all; he's just got issues. Zach is not a bad person, but he was obsessed with someone else, and I know as well as anyone that you cannot give new people a fair shot when completely absorbed by another. It's tempting to think, "I can make you forget all about her." Much to my dismay, this is impossible. However, it's no shortcoming of yours or mine. When a problem exists in someone's head, their head is the only place the problem can be solved. Come to think of it, believing you can solve other people's problems is also a problem. If the man is meant to go away, work on himself, and come back to you, then that is what will happen. You don't have to try and make arrangements for it to happen. If it's meant to be, it will be. In the meantime, he did you a favor.

In *The Mastery of Love* Don Miguel Ruiz further explains this favor: "Explore the possibilities. Be yourself. Find a person who matches with you. Take a risk, but be honest. If it works, keep going. If it doesn't work, then do yourself and your partner a favor: Walk away; let her go. Don't be selfish. Give your partner the opportunity to find what she really wants, and at the same time give yourself the opportunity. If it's not going to work, it is better to look in a different direction. If you cannot love your partner the way she is, someone else can love her just as she is. Don't waste your time, and don't waste your partner's time. This is respect." It doesn't feel like respect in the moment, I know. It feels like rejection. Accept that there are things about the situation that you don't know. Knowing what I know now, Zach did me a favor.

This is a type of respect that not everyone will show you, but you can show it to others and you can show it to yourself. Try not to use other people to heal your own hurt. If you do, you risk hurting another person and you prolong your own pain. Although it's difficult, try to work through the pain without a rebound relationship. Also, you can show this type of respect to yourself. If you want a relationship to go in one direction and he wants to go in another or is content standing still, walk away. Find someone who wants what you want. Yes it's easier said than done, but how many times have you looked back and been so grateful that things didn't work out with a certain guy or had a relationship end and realized it could have ended a lot sooner? The universe is looking out for us even if we don't agree with its methods.

By the time I reintroduced myself to Zach, I was finished playing the "What's wrong with me?" game, but imagine if I hadn't been. I would have criticized myself for falling short of his expectations when his disinterest had nothing to do with me. He dated multiple women but nothing worked because he had his own mental mess to clean up. Despite our not being a match, I appreciate him telling me he hopes I find happiness (and I hope he finds it, too). I'm starting to appreciate that it's okay to be grateful for the time you do spend with someone even if it doesn't amount to a grand future. Two enjoyable evenings and one remarkably considerate e-mail is a rewarding exchange in and of itself.

Love Jo all your days, if you choose, but don't let it spoil you, for it's wicked to throw away so many good gifts because you can't have the one you want.

—Louisa May Alcott, *Little Women*

ASTRONAUT ON A MISSION

On the night of February 4, 2007, a woman named Lisa Marie Nowak, in her early forties, decided to go for a joyride. For this journey, she packed latex gloves, a black wig, a BB pistol and ammunition, pepper spray, a hooded tan trench coat, a two-pound drilling hammer, and an eight-inch Gerber folding knife. She then set out for the nine-hundred-mile trip from Houston to Orlando. When she arrived at Orlando International Airport the next day, she followed her lover's new flame, Colleen Shipman, into the parking lot and attempted an attack. Shipman, sensing someone was following her, locked the car door in time. She rolled down the window a few inches to talk to her stalker, and Nowak sprayed pepper spray in the car. Shipman drove to the nearest security booth, and police were summoned. When the media learned of the story, they focused on one thing: She was wearing an adult diaper during the drive so she didn't have to stop along the way. Nowak denies that was the case.

It's just another day in the land of crazy, right? Except for one thing: Captain Lisa Marie Nowak was an astronaut. She wasn't a bitter barista or a disgruntled stripper. She was a U.S. Naval Flight Officer and a NASA astronaut with a master's in aeronautical engineering. At the time of the attack, she lived with her husband of nineteen years and their three children. She had no prior record of such behavior. Lisa is highly intelligent and socially adept, yet she was caught completely off guard by an unrequited obsession.

In 2004, Lisa began an affair with a man named William Oefelein shortly after his divorce; it went on for two years. He started to back away toward the end of 2006 and began seeing Colleen Shipman. Nowak was determined to put a stop to it. After the incident, NASA scrambled, asking, "Where did we go wrong in our screening process?" I don't think they did go wrong. If she'd never felt obsessive love before, this probably surprised her, too.

I asked Professor Wakin if he remembered the news story. He said yes and that he'd seen it before. Otherwise intelligent people fall apart in this one area and it affects all aspects of their lives—but fortunately not always to this extreme. He said, "Sometimes people are in a routine relationship for years, they meet someone, become addicted and risk everything." He told me the story of a judge, a man who was married with kids and considered a pillar in the community. He had a one-night stand with a woman at a law conference and subsequently developed an obsession with her. In the process, he lost everything and ended up disbarred and divorced. One of the symptoms of limerence is "Distractibility to the point where relationships and responsibilities are compromised."

Thankfully Nowak did not complete the Shipman mission—though not for lack of trying. Unfortunately she chose to go to Home Depot for the hammer and folding knife instead of seeking therapy.

If limerence, specifically, sounds like something you've experienced, Google "Love Variant Wakin-Vo." A paper Professor Wakin and his colleague Duyen B. Vo wrote on limerence will come up. There is also a link to the paper on the limerence Wikipedia page. Read through it for further description of the condition.

FIVE

REMOVE THE "TAKE ADVANTAGE OF ME" SIGN FROM YOUR BACK

Never allow someone to be your priority while allowing yourself to be their option.

—Mark Twain

Of all the pearls of wisdom found in *The Art of Loving*, this one sent my chin to the floor and kept it there for a good sixteen minutes: "If an individual is able to love productively, he loves himself too; if he can love *only* others, he cannot love at all." WHAT? But what about self-sacrifice and putting other people first? What about giving up everything in the name of love? You heard the man: ". . . if he can love *only* others, he cannot love at all." In other words, if the only trick you have up your sleeve is being nice to people just to get them to like you, then you've got nothing. If you do everything a guy wants, with little-to-no regard for your own needs, all in exchange for him occasionally saying, "Baby, you look pretty today," then what you share is less than love. Woman up! You are an integral part of your own life. How you feel about yourself is not up for discussion.

You probably know one or two people who *only* love others. They'll do anything anyone asks. It seems they were born without a backbone and can't bring themselves to say no. Most of us don't allow ourselves to be taken advantage of at all times and in all places, but we do when certain people are involved, and it's usually because we want something from them. We want to sit at the cool kids' table, and so we take the subtle ridicule. Or we want affection from some guy, and so we take the subtle (or not so subtle) ridicule, or the lack of communication, or the blatant flirting with other women. We convince ourselves this is the right course of action—we're just compromising—but it's really fear in kindness's clothing. It's the fear of losing his approval or of not being good enough for him. Yet somehow doing all those favors doesn't add up to him loving us; rather, it gives him permission to take advantage of us.

To be clear: Fromm (in *The Art of Loving*) says, "If an individual is able to love productively, he loves himself too," not . . . he loves himself only; there needs to be a balance between loving yourself and others. Someone else said this, too . . . who was it . . . oh yes, it was Jesus: "Love thy neighbor as thyself." We usually look to this passage for guidance on how we're meant to love others, but let's also look at it for direction in loving ourselves. If you're using "thyself" as a gauge for how much love to extend to your neighbor, then the love you have for yourself needs to be generous. We know that one extreme—only thinking of yourself—is narcissism, and we're so afraid of appearing narcissistic that we turn to the other, equally unhealthy extreme—only thinking of others.

Fear of narcissism is one of the reasons we're afraid to discuss self-love at all. We think they're one in the same, but, no—they are, in fact, radically different. A woman who loves herself and believes she's beautiful carries herself in a self-assured way. A deep breath is all she needs to feel a connection with her inner beauty, her inner self, and to receive a shot of love for the day. A woman who *does not* believe she's beautiful is the one who needs to hear all the time that she is. She seeks constant reassurance. People who cannot make her feel beautiful—because she doesn't think they are beautiful—are of no use to her. Whereas a woman who loves herself sees value in all people.

These are opposite ends of the spectrum and most of us find ourselves somewhere in the middle. To cross officially over to the self-love side of the street, check in with yourself often. Start with your vitals: Am I getting enough sleep? Eating well? Getting enough exercise? If no, then you've got your first priority. Ask yourself how you're feeling, and listen to the response. You may be telling yourself you need downtime (if you've over scheduled yourself) out-and-about time (if you've been antisocial lately) or new adventure time (if life feels a little predictable).

To take good care of yourself, sometimes you have to say no. You can't do everything for everyone else all the time. Sometimes you need an afternoon at the spa. Once you're in the habit of making sure your basic needs are met, you can ask yourself some more daring and ultimately satisfying questions such as, "Are there any risks I've been afraid to take?"

When you end up involved with a man (or man after man after man) who takes advantage of your good nature, it means his insecurities have spotted yours. Both parties are operating on neediness. He needs sex, maybe money, possibly a place to stay. You need to feel needed. You spend time with each other based on what you lack. A man who takes advantage of others isn't necessarily a bad person, he's a man who doesn't know himself. He's using you to mask his insecurities rather than facing up to them, and there's nothing you can do about it. You can't shake him and say, "Figure yourself out so we can be together." That's something he has to want to do, and he has to initiate the process on his own.

Likewise, a woman who allows herself to be taken advantage of repeatedly is one who is avoiding her true self. If you tend to your insecurities the way you tend to these men, your self-doubts will start to dissipate. Then miraculously you will stop attracting these types and/or you will possess the enchanted power to walk away from them so quickly, it's as if you were never there to begin with. A healthy relationship will come complete with your perspective and his; your needs will receive equal airtime.

All the mistakes I ever made in my life were when I wanted to say No, and said Yes.

—Moss Hart

FLATTERY AND RANDOM GIFT GIVING WILL GET YOU NOWHERE

I called a guy friend of mine one night and asked what he was up to. He said, dejectedly, "I'm drawing a picture of a cartoon donkey." I responded slowly, "Okay . . . why?" He confessed, "It was Karla's favorite cartoon as a kid so I'm drawing it . . . I know this isn't going to work, but I'm still doing it." Karla had blown my friend off several times. Tonight the plan was to draw the donkey—he's a talented artist—and show up at the bar where she worked to deliver it in a valiant gesture. I thought, That's really dumb . . . aaaaaaand I've done the same thing. Oh it's so much easier to see other people's gaffes than it is to see our own. My preferred method has been writing. My thinking went like this: I'll write him a letter—flatter him to pieces. It'll make him feel so good about himself that he'll want to receive such letters from me every day. Mind you, this has yet to work. It didn't work for my artist friend, either. Karla said thank you, as any human with a beating heart would, and went about her business of not returning his calls.

When things aren't going as planned with a person of desire, oftentimes we get this novel idea: "I know! I'll be nice to him. I'll be soooo nice. I'll be the nicest person there ever was, and that way he'll have to have me around because there's no one nicer." Alas, this can have the unintended effect of making us look, not nice, but needy. Going out of your way for someone who won't give you the time of day inadvertently gives him permission to take advantage of you, and it also sets you up to feel belittled by your own behavior. You convince yourself you're doing a selfless deed when really you're just making a covert attempt to get what you want.

When being nice to the umpteenth power doesn't produce the desired result, you may throw yourself a little pity party. For example, a girlfriend of mine was getting the cold shoulder from a man she'd been out with a few times. She knew he was going to Costa Rica, so she made him a mini–travel kit and dropped it off at his apartment. He wasn't home, so she left it with his roommate. At the end of the day when she hadn't received a thank-you text (or any text) from him, she was incensed. "This is who I am," she said to herself. "I'm just a nice person. What's wrong with being a nice person?!"

There's nothing wrong with being nice for the sake of being nice, but here's the catch: the wonderful thing about being a pleasant person is that it's a reward in and of itself. If you hold the door open for someone and a smile in exchange is all you need, you're good. Or if you do a friend a favor and know it'll come back to you in some way—but you don't care how or when—then all is well with your friendship. When you give gifts or do unrequested favors for someone you have feelings for, however, you're not doing it for nothing in return—you want *everything* in return. You want his attention. His affection. His undying love. You want him to know that you are the sweetest thing there ever was. Think about it: These gestures are more for you than it is for him.

Paradoxically, you improve your chances by walking away. My friend Lori met a hot guy at a wedding and they exchanged contact information, but he was pussyfooting around when it came time to make plans. She got sick of it and said, "Look I don't need a pen pal. Take care." He responded *immediately* with, "I'll call you this weekend." They gave it another go. They're married now. My Aunt Jennifer's boyfriend, George, broke up with her with the typical, "Let's be friends." She replied, "No, I have enough friends." A few weeks later he came back. They've been married for twelve years. For the record, walking away does NOT guarantee that he'll recant. As a matter of fact, I think these are special cases. Nine times out of ten, if he's not interested and you walk away, he will not follow.

This is a win-win, however—if you turn your back and it causes him to get his act together and come after you, great; if not, it frees you up to meet men who are interested. In either case, it keeps you from being his lackey.

At first, it's difficult to accept that being nice isn't going to get you what you want. A lot of what we're doing here is forgetting everything we knew to be true and reprogramming ourselves. It will feel like you're going against the grain initially, but if you stick with it, I guarantee you'll feel better about yourself. Next time you feel the urge to be super-duper nice with sprinkles on top to a man who is looking the other way, stop yourself and ask, *Why, exactly am I doing this?* I'm not suggesting that you be mean. Just be neutral and maybe a little cold— in the name of self-preservation—until he gives you reason to act otherwise. If you do feel the overwhelming desire to give gifts—give them freely and often to the people who have already made it clear they want you in their lives—not those whose love and/or friendship you hope to obtain. Your company is gift enough; if someone doesn't see that, then keep calm and carry on.

HAS ANYONE SEEN MY SELF-ESTEEM?

During the first decade of life—in some cases the first two— our sense of who we are comes from other people. It begins with parents, siblings, the bossy girl next door, or the kind boy down the street. During adolescence, approval shifts drastically away from the home front to the social circle. High school social experiences vary depending on which character you play— head cheerleader, drum major, Goth guy who does lighting for

the musicals, outcast in the corner—and this sets us on different paths toward self-esteem. Sometimes the outcasts are given
an advantage—though it doesn't seem so at the time. They
never had the crowd's approval to begin with, so they don't
bother seeking it. Others spend their entire lives losing sleep
over what the neighbors think.

Most of us, when we hit adulthood, don't crave the crowd's
opinion as much as we once did but we do select certain
people—whether we mean to or not—and seek their approval
like buried treasure. This is brought to life especially when
waiting for a certain someone to respond to an electronic message. You text a guy you worship or send an e-mail to the re-
cruiter of your dream job. You'd rather have someone take
your spleen out with a spoon than wait more than an hour to
hear back. Even an hour is pushing it, especially from the guy.
With this process, you've unknowingly put your self-worth into
a communication and sent it off to another. If they respond,
everything is okay—self-esteem was returned in a reasonable
amount of time. Otherwise, the internal forecast is cloudy with
a chance of low confidence.

Some excitement over a new job prospect is understandable;
giddiness over a new man, even more so. When your life is on
hold regularly, however, because you need another person's approval like oxygen, it's time to resuscitate yourself. It's true old
habits die hard, and we've been looking to others for validation
since day one, so this takes some resolve. First, ask yourself,
how did this one individual get so much power? This is *one
person* we're talking about—on a planet of billions—and he
has the power to pick you up and place you on cloud nine with

a measly text message or send you straight to the corner wearing a dunce cap. Where did such an almighty influence come from? You gave it to him. Yes, that is the only way he got it. The majority of the world's population goes about its day without giving a damn about this dude, and everyone gets along just fine. Yet you have chosen him to be the determiner of your self-worth, so you wait with bated breath for him to give you a little nugget of approval. Just an ounce is enough. Fortunately, since you were the one to give him this power, you can take it back.

Next time you find yourself counting those dreadful minutes, hours, days waiting for a reply, remind yourself that whether this person responds or not, you don't change. You have the same talents and insights you did this time last week. You can still recite the periodic table from memory, bake an amazing German chocolate cake, or play a mean ukulele. Take a second and acknowledge that you are physically okay and you haven't technically lost anything. Also, think about the fact that it isn't the person but what you think he has that's important to you—in the case of the job, a career opportunity; in the case of the man, the love you've been longing for. In which case I say again (forgive the repetition) that the only person who is going to make or break your life is you. An outside person can't take it all away unless you give him permission to do so. Never forget, there is always another possibility out there, so don't put all of yourself into this one opportunity, this one person.

Before sending out that important text or e-mail next time, ask yourself why you're sending it—do you have something valid to say or are you sending it just because you're hungry for attention and need the reply? To figure it out, ask yourself this: If I knew for certain that this person would not respond, would I still send the message? In some cases, the answer is yes. You think, This opportunity is important to me, and I'll sleep better knowing I did everything I could, or I have one last thing to say to this guy. In those instances, hit send and feel secure in your decision regardless of the outcome. Other times, when the only point of the message is to prompt a response, consider not clicking the Send button. Sometimes this action is just as bold as the opposite.

A few years ago I received a careless text from a guy I coveted. I had expected to hear from him much sooner and I said to myself, You know what, I'm not writing back. I know I won't hear from him again and that's that. It's about time. I spent a blissful weekend not checking my phone constantly. Unexpectedly, he wrote me on Monday and asked if I was okay. I was drawn back into the fold of him by his e-mail, but I had made an important first step. I realized that I had the strength to keep my self-worth with me for an entire weekend. Nothing happens overnight, and this was the first of many empowering baby steps. When it takes more energy to stop yourself from getting in touch with someone than it does to send another eager text, you know it's the right thing to do. You're one step closer to keeping your self-esteem with you at all times.

A frequent exchange of text messages is not a relationship. It's not even a pen pal.

—Ethlie Ann Vare, *Love Addict: Sex, Romance, and Other Dangerous Drugs*

THE DISAPPEARING/REAPPEARING MAN

I mentioned my friend Lori earlier—the brazen gal who told the guy she didn't need a pen pal. When John, her now husband, followed up that weekend, he entered her life once and for all. He called when he said he would. He always showed up on time. They lived three hours apart, so every weekend one of them was driving to see the other. After a bumpy start, the relationship transformed into something mutual and consistent. This is not to be confused with a man who gives you the runaround, comes back when he needs a little TLC, vanishes again, returns again after some other girl blows him off, and so on. Don't look for the silver lining, telling yourself, "But he keeps coming back to me!" You are one of his many ego boosters, and he'll dangle you as long as you let him. Cut the cord.

I was once telling a girlfriend about a man who didn't call me, and she interrupted with, "Don't you believe in second chances?" Yes, I believe in giving second chances to men who ask for second chances. This guy wasn't asking for a second chance; in fact, he wasn't even apologizing. It comes naturally to unrequited folk to hand out second-chance cards to men who haven't requested them. Here, I forgive you. The men look confused, almost as if to say, "What is this? I don't want this, but if you want to go down on me I won't stop you." It's easy to get caught in the disappearing/reappearing man cycle by saying to yourself, No one is perfect. He makes mistakes. It's true no one is perfect, and all relationships require compromise. You don't have to expect perfection of any man, but certainly expect a strong sense of "We're in this together" to know

if the relationship is on solid ground. A man who has no respect for what's going on in your life and only shows up when
it's convenient for him has no respect for you. Here are a few
ways to make the determination:

- **There Are No Mixed Signals:** Believing someone is
  sending mixed signals can keep you engrossed longer
  than necessary. It's much more fun to play the mixed-
  signal game than to make peace with someone not liking
  you—but the latter is ultimately better. If a guy likes you,
  his communication will be reliable.

- **Don't Make Plans with Invisible People:** When caught
  up in someone, it's easy to make "what if" plans. "I'll sit
  in tonight, because what if he calls." "I'll get ready now
  because what if he texts me at seven and wants to see me
  at seven thirty." Live your life and make your plans.
  Don't worry about what ifs. Only concern yourself with
  actual occurrences. If he calls and you're out with girlfriends, you'll call him back.

- **Don't Nurse His Broken Heart:** It's tempting, I know.
  He's so lonely and vulnerable, and you'll nurse his heart
  back to health so he can love you fully. Either that or he'll
  let you lick his wounds now and run right back to his ex
  the second she calls. The latter is 96.7 percent more likely.
  If you have it within you to be strictly a friend during
  this time, proceed with caution. I tried it once and it was
  still ugly. I resisted his come-ons—because they only

took place when he was drunk. When he wasn't drunk, he would get angry with me when I didn't give him the *exact* advice he wanted to hear. If you can't keep your clothes on around him, stay away. Tell him to give you a call once he's had a few weeks to himself. There's an excellent chance he won't take time to reflect or heal at all. It's likely he'll run into the arms of another woman. Let that be her problem.

• **Bait & Switch:** Beware—be very aware—of men who treat you badly and blame you for it. A friend of mine had been dating a guy for little over a month when things started to go south. They made plans three times—time and place had been established in each case—and three times he backed out a few hours before with a text. The third time she responded, "What the hell?" His retort went something like: "This has been the busiest week of my life [insert long list of excuses that make him the most put-upon person on the planet]. I think that is so inconsiderate, cold and out of line that we need to go our separate ways and not see each other anymore. Lose my number."

She was distraught that he thought she was inconsiderate, and she scrambled to apologize. My attempts to convince her she hadn't done anything wrong were in vain. She had every right to call him out on casting her aside for a third time. If he wanted to be with her he wouldn't have left her hanging. For argument's sake, however, let's say life really did swallow him. If he were

genuinely interested he would have been the one apologizing, "I know it's ridiculous that I've canceled so many
times. I'll come over tomorrow and make it up to you."
He was looking for an out; he found it, and blamed her.
Brilliant.

I met a man at a wedding once. Unfortunately, his
level of interest was greater than mine. He was in the
army and he called me the week after we met—from
Kuwait. He had been granted permission to leave the
war zone for two weeks to attend his brother's wedding.
We hung out at the wedding and had lunch before he
had to go back. As soon as he returned he called me—
from Kuwait! On his way back to, you know, WAR. As
we were speaking I accepted that I can no longer make
excuses for men who tell me they're too busy to call. Drat.

WISDOM OF A PLAYWRIGHT

The next time you find yourself waiting by the phone, desperate for a call or a text from an ever evasive man, there's only one
thing to do: Pretend like you're good friends with Noël Coward. Noël Peirce Coward (1899–1973) was an English man of
the theater—playwright, director, and actor. In 1956 he sent a
tough-love letter to his good friend, actress Marlene Dietrich.
Marlene was in the midst of a tumultuous love affair with actor
Yul "Curly" Brynner. She was in her mid-fifties at the time—
nineteen years older than her lover. Go Marlene. Unfortunately,
Yul didn't always treat Marlene very well. Noël, tired of seeing
his friend in emotional agony, sent her this wake-up call. If you
ever need it, it's all yours.

"Curly is attractive, beguiling, tender and fascinating, but he is not the only man in the world who merits those de-lightful adjectives.... Do please try to work out for yourself a little personal philosophy and DO NOT, repeat DO NOT be so bloody vulnerable. To hell with God damned "L'Amour." It always causes far more trouble than it is worth. Don't run after it. Don't court it. Keep it waiting off stage until you're good and ready for it and even then treat it with the suspicious disdain that it deserves.... I am sick to death of you waiting about in empty houses and apart-ments with your ears strained for the telephone to ring. Snap out of it, girl! A very brilliant writer once said (could it have been me?) 'Life is for the living.' Well that is all it is for, and living DOES NOT consist of staring in at other people's windows and waiting for crumbs to be thrown to you. You've carried on this whole in corner, overcharged, romantic, unrealistic nonsense long enough. Stop it Stop it Stop it. Other people need you . . . Stop wasting your time on someone who only really says tender things to you when he's drunk. . . . Unpack your sense of humor, and get on with living and ENJOY IT."

DON'T TAKE ANYTHING PERSONALLY—PART TWO

I wrote earlier of not taking things personally. It's a good plan, right? Instead of being a sponge and absorbing other people's bad moods, insults, and careless actions, you should wear a sexy suit made of invisible rubber. Other people's emotional at-tacks bounce right off you, and you continue on unharmed. I neglected to mention, however, that there's a catch. In order to reap the full benefits of not taking anything personally, you can't take *anything* personally—even good things. In *The Four Agreements*, Don Miguel Ruiz says, "Whatever people do, feel, think or say, *don't take it personally*. If they tell you how wonderful you are, they are not saying that because of you. You know you are wonderful. It is not necessary to believe other people who tell you that you are wonderful."

Allow me to elaborate. Imagine you're scouring your closet for something to wear and you hate everything you see. You've worn all of these clothes dozens of times, *Why isn't there anything new in my closet?!* The clock is ticking and you begrudgingly grab that old green dress just so you're not late for work. You step into the elevator and someone says, "That's a pretty color." You say thank you and think, Maybe the color hasn't faded as much as I thought. You go into the kitchen for coffee and a coworker exclaims, "Great dress! I wish I could wear that length." By lunchtime four people have praised a dress that you were ready to put in the garbage disposal this morning. What started out as a dreary day has taken a turn onto Sunshine Blvd.

At first glance, nothing seems amiss here; it's a common occurrence. Look closer, though. What just happened? You gave other people complete control over how you feel about yourself. This doesn't seem like a bad thing when the influence lifts you up, but it's a one-way street. There is no, "I'll take the compliments but not the insults." If you allow other people to influence you for the better, you automatically let them influence you for the worse. What if you leave the house loving the outfit you have on and the same coworker remarks, "It's a little casual for work, don't you think?" Your delight turns to self-consciousness for the rest of the day.

When people compliment you, by all means say thank you. Politeness is recognizing that someone has extended a kindness to you. In your own mind, however, remind yourself that someone already confirmed that the dress was cute; you did—when you bought it. Part of the reason taking things personally is best avoided is because we can never know the source of the comment. Maybe, "I like your dress," is a genuine compliment. Maybe it's meant to fill the air during an awkward elevator ride. Perhaps this person just wants you to like her. Your cube mate might also be mocking you with a smile—à la Regina George in *Mean Girls*. There's no way to know for certain, so try not to allow your mood to rise and fall with others' remarks.

Let's look at this the unrequited way. You're out one night feeling undesirable and antisocial, but you promised a friend you'd accompany her, so you stay. To your surprise you meet a man, and what a man he is. Not only is he a pleasure to look at, but he also says the most thoughtful things. Things like, "You walk in beauty like the night of cloudless climes and starry skies and all that's best of dark and bright meet in your aspect and your eyes."* In other words, you're gorgeous, knowledgeable, and your eyes are stunning all in one sentence. If that's not what you want to hear, he can do better. "I can't get over how much you look like Adriana Lima" or "I never expected to

---

* First line of a Lord Byron poem called "She Walks in Beauty." He was quite the ladies' man.

have such an insightful conversation in a bar." Weeks go by and he provides a steady stream of compliments. Nothing goes unnoticed. He comments not only on the dress you're wearing but the way it hugs your hips. He openly appreciates being in the company of such a witty woman. Everything you ever wanted to believe about yourself is finally true because he says so.

Then one day, the compliments stop. He might be going through something at work and isn't able to give you as much attention. You're sympathetic with what he's going through but you'd like him to snap out of it. You need your sweet nothings like morphine. Or in another scenario, maybe he's more the malicious type. You've done something to piss him off, so he keeps the words you like to hear to himself because he knows you want them and this gives him some control over you. You'll do anything you can just to get him to be his poetic self again. And worse than keeping compliments to himself, he gets angry and insults you, "You're so stupid. You don't turn me on anymore."

If he stops telling you that you're incredible, does it stop being true? Did your IQ decrease? Your eyes, are they no longer blue? That's up to you. What if you believe at all times and in all places that you are clever, cute, and kind? You meet the same man in a bar, but instead of letting him convince you that you are attractive and intelligent, he confirms what you already know to be true. You both agree that you're a good catch. You both agree that he's a good catch. These are important things to have in common. Time goes by, you get comfortable and if he's in a bad mood and not up for reciting poetry, your self-esteem doesn't suffer. If he needs someone to talk to, he has you.

If he needs to process what he's going through alone, then you can leave him to himself without thinking there's anything wrong with you or your relationship.

Taking verbal abuse personally causes us to internalize negativity, which weighs us down emotionally. Taking praise personally opens us up to being taken advantage of and can result in an inflated sense of self. When talking about this with others, the fear most often expressed is that by not taking things personally we will alienate our fellow human beings. However, you can recognize and outwardly appreciate that someone says or does something thoughtful without letting it change how you feel about yourself. That's what taking things personally means—allowing the opinions of others to change the way you see yourself.

No doubt, not taking things personally is difficult, especially the accolades (those are things we want to hear, after all). It takes practice. I've mastered not taking certain things certain people say personally, but other things I continue to absorb; there's still work to be done. You can also say, "I'm not there yet. I recognize it's a good idea, but I'm not there yet." Simply recognizing it's a good idea will steer your subconscious toward trying it out some time. The first time it happens is marvelous. You tell yourself, "She just said something completely uncalled for. But wait, I don't care!" By not taking compliments personally you are less likely to fall for lines. Your bullshit meter will be in mint condition. You will discover sooner rather than later whether a man is worth getting to know or if he's all fluff 'n stuff.

I hold that it is none of my business what people think of me.

—Ashley Judd

THE LITTLE MERMAID

Selecting movies as a child was easy. There was no need to see previews or read reviews; my sister and I would march directly to the kids' section of the West Coast Video and judge movies based entirely on their colorful covers. We also didn't need to discuss much; I was the big sister and she usually agreed with my choices. One night I selected a movie called *The Little Mermaid*. This was a few years before the Disney version came out. I don't know who made it. If memory serves it was a Japanimation-type cartoon. Before the movie begins, there's an introduction praising the man who wrote the story: Hans Christian Andersen—Danish author of countless children's stories including *The Emperor's New Clothes, The Little Match Girl*, and *The Princess and the Pea*.

Since my very first viewing of *The Little Mermaid* I've known two things: 1. Who wrote it and 2. It's not a happily-ever-after story. Here's a synopsis of the original version:

The Little Mermaid (LM) saves the prince from drowning. She brings him to shore, but he never sees her. She swims away before he wakes. Another woman passing by sees him lying on the beach and runs to his "rescue." He sees that woman when he opens his eyes. LM makes a deal with the sea witch. She gives up her enchanting voice so she can become human—the catch is that she has to get the prince to marry her. Otherwise, at dawn the day after he marries another woman, LM will disintegrate into sea foam. The prince likes LM very much even though she can't speak. One day the prince's father orders his son to marry the neighboring king's daughter. The prince tells LM that the only woman he'll ever love is the one who rescued him from drowning but adds that the LM is beginning to take her place in his heart.

Under his father's insistence the prince goes to meet the neighboring princess. Guess who it is? Same girl who found him on the shore. The wedding is announced. The prince and princess marry, and LM's heart shatters. Before dawn, however, LM's sisters bring her a knife that the sea witch has given them in exchange for their long hair. If LM slays the prince and lets his blood drip on her feet, she will become a mermaid again. She walks quietly into the bedroom where the prince and princess are deep in post-coital sleep. She lifts the knife but she cannot bring herself to kill the prince. As dawn breaks, she throws herself into the sea.

When this was first published, in 1837, Anderson received criticism because the ending was so miserable. He later changed it so that instead of dissolving into sea foam the mermaid became a daughter of the air—in other words, she obtained a soul. At some point earlier in the story her grandmother tells her that merfolk don't have souls, only humans do. The daughters of the air blessed her since she wanted so badly to become human. I only remember her turning into sea foam in the version I saw. I also don't recall thinking the story was sad. As children, we don't necessarily form opinions about the stories we're told until later.

More than anything, I think this story is a commentary on the unfairness of love. Think about it: there's no one to blame; the prince doesn't technically do anything wrong. He tells LM upfront that the only woman he'll ever love is the one who rescued him from drowning. The fact that she doesn't have a voice to explain that she rescued him is, yes, maddening, as is the fact that he actually encounters the woman again. LM not having a voice is a metaphor for those in unrequited love not knowing how to speak up for themselves. The princess who rescues the prince knows nothing of LM, she only knows she found a handsome man dying on the shore one day, gives him mouth to mouth, and comes across him again a couple months later. Why not marry him? Surely it's destiny. We could blame the sea witch—knowing exactly the trouble she was causing taking away LM's voice, but what else could we expect from a woman who calls herself a witch.

Then there's the noble ending. Yes, it's noble. If we're going with this fatalistic version of the story then not killing the prince is the right thing to do. If she had killed him, then she would have learned what she felt for him was not love but a will to possess. Plenty of people think this way: *If I can't have you then no one can!* That's ownership. It's the ego insisting on its own way. Love finds a genuine way to handle whatever circumstance it is presented with, which is what LM did. I'd like to think I wouldn't kill the prince either, but I would wake him up. "Do you see this knife?" I would ask. "I am choosing NOT to kill you with this knife—even though it would guarantee my life!" Oh that's right, she couldn't talk. Dammit. I guess Hans told this story exactly the way he meant to.

I was ten years old in 1989 when Disney's *The Little Mermaid* was released. By that point, I had a firm understanding of the Disney brand and I also knew the original story's ending. "How are they going to make that work?" I wondered. Forgive me for ever doubting Disney's ability to airbrush over anything. Don't get me wrong, I like Disney's *The Little Mermaid* primarily for its supporting characters; namely, Scuttle the random seagull and Sebastian the condescending Jamaican crab. The music is spectacular and the animation top notch. Just remember: behind every seemingly perfect fairytale is an original script with a drastically different story to tell.

THE MAN BEHIND THE MERMAID

One day my fingers went walking over to *The Little Mermaid* Wikipedia page to compare my first-time Little Mermaid experience with the actual story. I recalled the broad strokes of the tale fairly well, but there was one detail I forgot—or it wasn't included in the movie I saw to begin with. Aside from losing her voice, the sea witch insists that LM make another sacrifice. "Drinking the potion will make her feel as if a sword is being passed through her, yet when she recovers she will have two beautiful legs, and will be able to dance like no human has ever danced before. However, it will constantly feel like she is walking on sharp swords hard enough to make her feet bleed most terribly. The Little Mermaid drinks the potion and meets the prince, who is mesmerized by her beauty and grace even though she is mute. Most of all he likes to see her dance, and she dances for him despite her suffering excruciating pain." Holy heart failure, Batman. The man who wrote this knows unrequited love, and he knows it very well. The overall story indicates a writer familiar with unreciprocated longing, but that detail took it to a whole new level of anguish. I decided to look in on the life of our courageous children's author.

Hans Christian Andersen (1805–1875) was born to impoverished parents in the small town of Odense, Demark. He was shy, effeminate, and unattractive (kind of like an ugly duckling). He left home at the age of fourteen with the hopes of becoming an actor in Copenhagen, but it turned out not to be his calling. A wealthy benefactor took a liking to him, paid for him to go to school, and helped launch his writing career. As a writer, Andersen wrote plays, poems, and novels, but he didn't receive acclaim until he began writing children's stories. Fairytales brought him worldwide recognition. In 1844 he said of his own life, "Twenty-five years ago, I arrived with my small parcel in Copenhagen, a poor stranger of a boy, and, today, I have drunk chocolate with the Queen, sitting opposite her and the King at the table." The Danish government paid him an annual stipend simply for being a national treasure.

His love life was not as enchanted. Andersen was attracted to both men and women, and he had a penchant for unattainable individuals regardless of sex. In 1840 he met and fell for Swedish Opera singer Jenny Lind. Her feelings were platonic, and she wrote him, "God bless and protect my brother is the sincere wish of his affectionate sister." What Jenny didn't give in affection she gave in inspiration—shortly after meeting her he wrote four of his most popular tales: *The Ugly Duckling, The Nightingale, The Snow Queen,* and *The Fir Tree.* When he died, Andersen was holding a lengthy letter from the unrequited love of his youth, a girl named Riborg Voigt. He left his entire estate to yet another unrequited love—Edvard Collin, his benefactor's son. A June 2005 article from *The Telegraph* says, "His diaries and notebooks indicate that he was terrified by and ashamed of sex; he probably died a virgin."

Poor Hans. I want to give him a hug and hand him a prescription for Lexapro. Since I can't do either, I'll just write him a little note:

Sweet Storyteller,

As children we are entertained by your stories only to realize as adults how tragically accurate they can be. Your grasp on the human experience was impressive. You lived in a time when the downtrodden were rarely educated. When you received your education, you did the most generous thing with it: you let other outcasts know they are not alone. While you never knew the reciprocated love of one person, you experienced a love that most others will never know— the official love of your country and the enduring love of the audience. Not just any audience—children. You gave personal power to the most powerless. Your stories are alive today on the page, on the stage, and on screen, big and small. I hope that your soul, like the Little Mermaid's, has found solace. On behalf of all the ugly ducklings and little mermaids of the world, thank you.

It doesn't matter if you're born in a duck yard, so long as you are hatched from a swan's egg!

—Hans Christian Andersen

SIX

ENCOUNTERS OF THE UNREQUITED KIND

so fuck you
and your untouchable face
and fuck you
for existing in the first place
and who am i
that i should be vying for your touch
and who am i
i bet you can't even tell me that much
—Ani DiFranco, from the song "Untouchable Face"

Unrequited love is all about planning. The fact that these plans aren't always based in reality aside, there's still some serious planning going on; planning for a future that he isn't onboard with—yet. Planning to find out what he did last night by asking around or social media investigating. Planning to see him. This last one is the quintessential unrequited experience that can be both planned and accidental at the same time. You can arrange to be where he'll be and look stunning, but there are factors that cannot be accounted for—such as Prince Caspian showing up with a female companion.

Let's look at the two types of unrequited encounters—the surprise run-in and the orchestrated run-in. Since we're talking about planning, we'll discuss the orchestrated run-in first. To clarify, orchestrated run-ins don't necessarily mean balls-to-the-wall stalking. They're when you either know someone's patterns because you work together, go to school together, or frequent the same bar, and you position yourself to be somewhere when you think he'll be there. Or you do some light social media stalking: you hadn't planned to go to a party but you see he responded yes to the Evite and you rearrange your life to be there. That's the orchestrated run-in.

If you're devising run-ins it means you're still holding out hope to be with this man. I'm not saying it's right or wrong, but in the name of being honest with yourself, best to fess up that that's what's happening. I point it out in case you're doing it on autopilot and pretending you're not part of the process at all. "It's so strange," you might say, "we just keep running into each other." I, myself, have arranged plenty of run-ins, and when I was finally able to say to myself, "I'm done—I'm not trying anymore," the need to predict his next three steps became null and void. Coordinated encounters never work out the way they do in your head, so I decided to give control back to the gods.

As you know, the gods do exert this control every now and then and organize an unexpected meeting with your intended. I've had it happen in all ways—when I looked good, not so good, when I was feeling jovial and wanted to update someone on my life, and when I just wanted out of the conversation altogether. While it's nice to run into an old someone when you're on the arm of a new someone, it can be a superficial comfort. Having a person by your side doesn't necessarily mean you've moved on (or that your ex has moved on). That person might be a decoy—distracting even you from your honest feelings. The opposite is also true. Being at the party alone doesn't mean you haven't moved on. Your professional self, your amateur athlete or your spiritual self might be feeling fabulous. If you run into an ex, try not to be distracted by what things appear to be. Stay with yourself during the conversation; if you've got good news to share—share freely. If you don't, no need to lie or exaggerate. You're doing well; that's all.

In another scenario, perhaps he's on the arm of someone new; this is especially difficult. Or maybe she's not new, but the ex he left you for. It's a blunt object to the face either way. Again, I know what it looks like; it looks like he wins because two are better than one. Unless, that is, the one keeps her composure like nobody's business. When running into an ex or going to the guillotine, let dignity be your default setting. Marie Antoinette is said to have gone to her beheading with a dignity that infuriated her enemies. They wanted to see her squirm, and she denied them that satisfaction. You can make a strong statement just by keeping it together under pressure, but don't do it just to make other people wriggle. Do it because it feels incredible to be in control rather than at the mercy of public opinion.

Now is a good time to remind yourself not to take anything personally. You don't know what's happening. Maybe they're having a great night; or maybe she's about to deny him sex because she doesn't like the way he's looking at you. You don't know. You are simply three people who are going to converse for as long or as short a time as you decide. If you're feeling tender and it's difficult for you to stay at the party while they're there, leave. Don't make a scene—grab a good friend and go to the next party or home or wherever you think the best place is. If you want to stay just to try and interrupt their evening, then you're operating under the orchestrated run-in clause, i.e., you haven't given up. In that case, that very moment would be a good time to give up (on him not on love). He's there with someone else.

DRESS REHEARSAL

Whether he's a recent ex or an object of active yearning, the possibility of running into him lends itself to needing a script. Even if the forecast says the chances of seeing him are next to none, it can be a preoccupation, wherein you say to yourself, I need to know *exactly* what I'm going to say if I EVER run into him again. So we rehearse—in our heads or out loud. Not only the words but also the inflection and sometimes the facial expressions need to be just right. The trouble is, you can know exactly what you're going to say—have it memorized, notarized, or emblazoned on a plaque, but it will leave your head like a rodent caught by a flashlight the moment you see him. Even if you do manage to say exactly what you had planned, his reaction will not be what you imagined. It might be better or it might be worse, but it won't play out as you thought it would.

Knowing there's a good chance that all of the rehearsing will be for naught, let's come up with an alternate plan. Instead of pinpointing exactly what you're going to say, think instead about what you'd like your position to be. For example, let's say you want to be polite but have the conversation end quickly. Perhaps you want to be cold and have the conversation end before it begins. (Take note: being cold is different than being mean. Being cold says I acknowledge you're here but I don't care to interact. You can be cold and still keep it together. There is no dignity in being mean.) Accept in advance that things will mostly likely be awkward and that's the way it goes. There will be all kinds of things not being said—a parade of pink elephants going by, which everyone here knew already. If all other thoughts and words flee, remember only these two: Stay calm. Let everything flow from there.

You can also let the moment be the moment. Let this moment, when he's not here, be, and let the moment you see him, if and when it arrives, be. You may find you're up for a conversation, which is fine, or you may find you're not, also fine. Maybe in talking to him you'll have the sudden and extraordinary realization that you are no longer attracted to him. Cue the hallelujah chorus. Or maybe seeing him will awaken feelings you thought were dormant, in which case, you can excuse yourself to go do that thing. Perhaps this is the gratifying moment when you realize that a friendship is possible. Let the moment tell you what to do and don't suffer needless anxiety beforehand.

As for the need to rehearse—realize that there's more going on than just wanting to know what to say. You're processing— either the attraction or the breakup. Every time you feel an impromptu rehearsal coming on, write it down. Write down what you want to say and maybe even how you envision the scene going. We go through many scripts in these uncertain emotional times. Process it for your sake, not for the sake of the possible run-in. As you write, try to assess where you are with the whole thing. "I'm not over him yet and I don't want to be. I think there's still a chance." "I'm not over him but am so ready to be!" "I feel over it but the need to have some sort of revenge hasn't gone away." Let self-honesty be your guide. A few writing sessions might be just the thing you need to end the dress rehearsal and focus on the now-playing production that is your very own life.

PRESENTING YOUR CASE—WITHOUT HOPE OR AGENDA

Once upon a time writer/director Richard Curtis decided to gather all the well-known actors in the land (Eng-land) and throw in an American or three—Billy Bob Thornton, Laura Linney, with a cameo by Denise Richards. He stirred them all together and out came the Christmas movie *Love Actually*, a mingling of tales both absurd and touching. There are all kinds of love: love that smells like fresh-baked bread; love that's dry and crusty; platonic love; illegal love; and the recent loss of love. For added flavor there is unrequited love, and somewhere in the middle of this movie is one of the greatest unreciprocated love confessions that holiday cinema has ever seen.

Mark, played by English actor Andrew Lincoln, loves Juliet, played by Keira Knightly. Unfortunately Juliet just married Mark's best friend Peter. Mark does his best friend a solid by pretending he doesn't like Juliet at all—even in passing. Juliet—eager to endear herself to her husband's friend—stops by Mark's apartment unannounced and asks to see the video he made of their wedding. Mark tries to stop her from searching, but she sees the video and pops it in. As the footage rolls she realizes all the shots are of her. Mark watches helplessly as his secret spills in slow motion. Several scenes later, Mark decides to own his feelings. He shows up at Juliet and Peter's apartment one night. Poetic license ensures that Juliet, not Peter, answers the door. Without saying a word and with "Silent Night" playing in the background, Mark confesses his love to his best friend's wife using a series of flash cards that read:

> "But for now let me say,
> without hope or agenda
> just because it's Christmas
> (and at Christmas you tell the truth)
> to me you are perfect
> and my wasted heart will love you
> until you look like this . . . [*shows image of a mummy*]
> Merry Christmas"

As Mark leaves, Juliet runs after him and gives him an empathetic kiss. He continues on and says to himself, "Enough. Enough now." Earlier we touched on presenting your interest to a crush. Sometimes it's too late—a crush is a happy memory and searing love is the daily reality. This is the type of unrequited encounter you arrange as much for yourself as for the object of affection. You admit your love not because you think the other person will say it back but because it's the truth and what else is there to do with the truth but tell it. Mark knew that Juliet didn't feel the same, but he saw this as a way to flatter the woman he loved while ideally helping himself move on.

In late 2006 Jack—he of the magnificent muttonchops—
was in my apartment. We had been in e-touch for a few months,
and he stopped by on his way home from a business trip. By
this point he was engaged to the woman he had gotten back
together with after dating me. Over e-mail he confessed his
doubts. "We moved in together and all we did was fight. She
kept asking why we weren't engaged, so I asked her to marry
me hoping it would fix our problems. It didn't." I kept to myself
that I had read about that exact same scenario in an issue of
*Psychology Today.** I hear it's common.

We had come back from dinner and now there were two
choices: get naked or say good-bye. I was firm in my not getting
naked stance; I purposefully hadn't shaved my legs to keep myself in check. Still, we couldn't resist a minor make-out session,
from which I cautiously backed away. He didn't come after me
and I was grateful. When I say come after me, I mean in the
eager teenaged boy sense: "C'mon. C'mon. Nobody's watching." We were quiet and the room was filled with impossibility.
By way of explaining that I wanted to sleep with him but wasn't
going to I said, "The problem here is that I love you." It was the
truth as far as I knew it. I thought about him every day.

He turned to me slowly with his forehead wrinkled in as-
tonishment. I knew he wouldn't say it back. It would have been
disingenuous if he had. We paused for a moment, talked about
how long it would take him to get home, and then we knew it
was time to say good-bye. I walked him to his car. Nice things
were said, but we knew nothing would top my confession, and
so we didn't try too hard. Heading back to my place, I feared I

* "The Perils of Playing House," July 2005; available online for free

wouldn't sleep. I slept ever so soundly, though, as I no longer had anything to be afraid of. So what if I never hear from him again, I thought, I've already dealt with that.

He wrote me the next day with more than I expected, saying, "About the love thing. I thought that I loved [insert fiancée's name] but something inside says that might not be so. The thing that scares me is that I might not know exactly what love is but when I'm with you I might just find out." This was music to my well-rested ears—for a few days. I soon learned, however, that he said these things occasionally but never did anything about them. I'm sure at the time I thought, Of course I can show you what love is. But the truth is, I could not. I could not show him what love is and neither could she. Only he can. Only he can find out who he is and what loves means to him. If he does, he will be better equipped to decide who he wants to spend the rest of his life with.

Jack continued on his ever-doubting way and sat on my couch a month before the wedding with his head in his hands saying, "I can't do it." I said, "Don't do it, then." He replied in frustration, "I have to. I'm too far in now." In my opinion, he was right. It's more tragic to call off a wedding that's already been planned than to get divorced a few years later—at least in our society—because that's where we place the emphasis, on the wedding, not the marriage. It was the last time I saw him. Both of us knew we had no business being in touch, but neither of us was willing to cut the cord, so fate did it for us.

A few days after our couch conversation, I wrote him. The theme of my e-mail was, "You're about to take vows you don't mean." He called in reply and said, "I know. I'm just gonna be that guy." "What guy?" I asked. "The guy who gets divorced."

I had no response to such a sentence. If that's where his head was, so be it. Two weeks later he wrote me saying we couldn't be in touch anymore. Apparently, he was rereading my e-mail when his computer froze. He turned it off. His fiancée turned it back on a short while later and, "You're about to take vows you don't mean," was front and center. He begged me not to tell her how long we had been in touch if she e-mailed me directly (she never did) and added that he realized he truly loved her. That was that.

Back in those days I went to MySpace for my cyber surveillance. Looking at his wedding photos didn't hurt—maybe because I knew firsthand of the uncertainty behind those cinnamon-brown eyes. In an attempt to be positive, I relayed to a guy friend of mine how happy they looked. He chimed in with perfect sarcasm, "Really? They looked happy in their *wedding* photos. So did John Wayne Gacy!"*

I don't believe in saying, "I thought I loved you but I was wrong." Love is an infinite concept. It means something different to each person and changes definition throughout one's life. Years later you might look back and realize what you felt was puppy love, obsessive love, or something less than the love you know now. But if you thought it was love at the time, it was. It was love in the shallow end of the pool. Looking back, I remember telling Jack I loved him as a genuine and brave moment for me. I found it fascinating that I was more certain about wanting to be with him than he was about being with the woman he was going to marry. I see now that my certainty

* John Wayne Gacy was a serial killer convicted of murdering thirty-three young men. He was married twice.

was as dangerous as his uncertainty. I watched him waver on this crucial life decision and still just wanted him to pick me rather than see the red flag of instability and run. Good thing the universe knew better. Six years and no children later, Jack is still married. It's all I know. It's all I care to know. It's all I have any business knowing.

If you had an opportunity to declare love to someone and didn't take it, there's no need to regret it. The way I see it, you have two choices: Confess now (people are easy to find these days) or let it go, but don't be endlessly remorseful. A girlfriend of mine kicks herself repeatedly for not telling a man she worked with that she had feelings for him. She's convinced if she had, he would've moved out of his girlfriend's place and in with her. I've told her that, yes, there is a feeling of courage that comes with confessing, but it's unlikely to change the situation. She won't hear it, though. I think in a way she's glad she didn't do it, so she can always tell herself it would have worked out.

In the end, it's best to reconcile yourself to the fact that you can't go back; you can only take what you've learned and apply it to situations if and when they present themselves again. If you choose to confess, be aware that you might catch the object of your affection off guard, so try to pick an appropriate moment—preferably, when the two of you are alone and no alcohol is involved. If he's attached to someone, acknowledge that fact so it doesn't seem like you're making a play.

DIGITAL RENDEZVOUS

One July evening at 7:41 p.m. in the year of our Lord 2008, my friend Karina sent me the following text message: "You'll never guess who's sitting next to me at Café Noir. That's right! Indiana Jones. He's with some blonde talking about Bali. Of course he's doing all the talking and the girl's just shaking her head . . . Yes. Haven't heard her say one word yet. Haha!"

This is the twenty-first century's distinctive way of running into someone. You don't even have to be there. I don't recall if I responded to Karina. My immediate thought was, "I have to write that down because I'm going to use it someday" (writer's logic). Once that task was finished, I was amused. In one short message she gave a spot-on summary of this guy. Café Noir, Bali, blonde—yeah that's him. Plus there was the entertaining detail that his date was staying silent. A well-crafted text message, my friend. If I did respond, it was a one-liner. We didn't have an exchange.

This text didn't hurt, it just irked me a little. I already knew Indiana to be a—how shall we say—man about town. Karina wasn't the first of my friends to run into him on a date. Had I not had a sense of his gamesmanship, however, then it would have undoubtedly left me distraught. It's difficult, not to mention completely unnatural, to know exactly where a guy you like—or once liked—is at that moment and have a loose description of who he's with while you're home folding laundry. It's better left unknown, yet I don't begrudge my friend for sharing. I would have done the same.

This is like Facebook stalking in that the information is there if you want it, but so is the self-control. Although tempting, it's best not to get into a question/answer session—you risk setting your cognition ablaze. Don't ask, "What's she wearing? What are they talking about? Is she pretty? Prettier than me?" In doing so you're trying to become a part of what's happening, and you can't be. No matter how much information you gather, you cannot change the situation. Even if you get dressed and show up, they'll still fall for each other (if that's what was going to happen anyway) and they'll have that funny memory about the loony girl who tried to sabotage their date. Does it suck? Royally. Is it unfair? Tremendously. Can you change it? Not without doing something illegal. If you ever find yourself in this situation, simply text your friend: "Thanks for the update. Please ignore him and enjoy yourself!"

If you find this real-time information hurtful, there's only one thing to do: be sad. Be disillusioned, frustrated, or annoyed. Whatever you need to feel. Call a friend—one who is not sitting at the table next to Tarzan and Jane. I know that's probably not the answer you were hoping for; after all, we prefer answers to relationship questions that don't involve being emotionally inconvenienced. *Sad? Why would I want to feel that?* Because experiencing our emotions is hard, many of our actions—like showing up at the bar or texting our friend for every detail—are meant to avoid misery. It never works, though, at least not in the long term; instead, it's better to face up to your feelings. Not that you actively want to feel bad, but all of our emotions serve a purpose and when one of them wants to commune with you, let it. You can avoid sadness by showing up or asking for details or drinking yourself into oblivion, but it will be waiting for you when you wake up. You can spend the next day shopping yourself into serious debt, hoping that'll do the trick. Sadness will hang out on the hammock until you get home. It's a persistent little bastard. Whatever emotion comes knocking, let it in. Feel it now and be done. Avoid it and the fear of feeling it grows stronger and the attempts to evade it become more creative.

While you're sitting at home being sad and the two of them are out laughing and listening to him talk, it feels like it will be this way forever. Them happy, you sad. I promise it won't. There will come a day when you're exceedingly happy and one, or both, of them will be depressed. But you won't know about it and, more important, you won't care. We all go through emotional cycles and seasons. No one gets a perpetual pleasure pill. You may have thought he was that pill—the everlasting gobstopper. I thought Indiana was. But happiness is not one person. It's not even one emotion. Happiness is the productive processing of all emotions. Stay in with your sadness, have a cup of tea or a glass of wine (just one), or find a friend to lean on. Watch a Will Ferrell movie on Netflix or pop in that multi-disc set of *Pride & Prejudice* that's been sitting on your shelf. Be kind to yourself and indulge your whims—at least a few of them. Start over tomorrow.

ALL HALLOWS' EVE

There is one other holiday—in addition to New Year's Eve—when the island of Manhattan sticks its collective finger in the electric socket: the nontheistic night of Halloween. Like New Year's, it's a mission impossible to hail a cab, and there are puddles of vomit in every subway car. What's different is that the whole country watches New York as the year turns, while Halloween is for the locals.

I was in New York and loving my costume on All Hallows' Eve 2008. Last-minute costumes often end up being ill-fitting and feeling wrong, but this was a good one. I was a Geisha wearing a very short kimono and fishnet stockings. A high current coursed through me because there was a strong possibility that someone—the aforementioned character Indiana Jones—might be at the club I was heading to.

Indiana and I had had plans to meet up the weekend before that night, but I bailed. I canceled because I figured our getting together would look like it had many times before. We spent weekends together that were wonderful from my vantage point. Our liaison was a vibrant mix of drinks, dinner parties, righteous make-out sessions, compelling conversation, savory sleep during which he held onto me all night, and sex. Heaven help me, the sex. Let's just say there were a lot of I-can't-believe-we're-fucking-for-the-fifth-time-today moments. Our chemistry was cerebral, sexual, alive and well.

At the end of said weekends, I would usually present him with the possibility of us doing this regularly. I felt no shame in asking. The man put on a good show of enjoying my company, after all. But his answer was always the same—never a flat-out no; more of a roundabout one. One reply was, "I want this and I want it with you, but I also don't want this." I only heard the first half of that sentence. Another time it was, "It's difficult not to consider when there's this much chemistry." You don't say. I wrote him an e-mail at one point confessing that it was time for me to put my emotional white flag up in surrender. He wrote back and invited me to his office Christmas party.

When I made my final recommendation that we be together, he declared, "The fact is that I'm un-datable." That statement didn't contradict his lifestyle; I knew he dated. A lot. I envied it. He seemed able to do what I couldn't—have fun with dating. I was also envious because I knew if he ever wanted to get married all he'd have to do is roll out the door and smile at the next pretty passerby. But I digress. We had tentative plans to spend what was sure to be another lascivious weekend in each other's company, and I decided I wasn't going to do it again. Ambiguity means no. I wrote, told him I couldn't make it, and hoped the universe would give me points for doing the right thing.

Running into him, however, was entirely different. If the fates decided we were going to be at the same place at the same time, so be it. As my girlfriends and I walked to the club I repeated to myself, *Flirting, no sex. Flirting, no sex. Maybe making out, no sex. Making out, no sex.* The scene was a cavalcade of costumes. There was a girl dressed as Rollergirl from the movie *Boogie Nights.* Committed to her character, she was on the dance floor in skates—highly impressive. There were fairies, witches, wenches, and everyone looked the part. New Yorkers take this holiday very seriously. I was at the club for about an hour when a mutual friend Indiana and I shared left, so I figured game over. Indy wasn't coming. I was relieved and disappointed at the same time.

A short while later, I was refilling my champagne glass when someone tapped me on the shoulder. I turned, not knowing what to expect, and there he was—tall, dark, and delicious. I was caught off guard both by the fact that he was there—I had already made my peace with him not coming—and that my attraction continued to be a life force of its own. My instant thought: How could I not sleep with him? I mean gravity is gravity. If he falls on the floor and I fall on top of him there's really nothing anyone can do about it. Plus, we were in costume, for the love of paganism. That's one kind of sex we hadn't had.

Then he introduced me to his date. I didn't notice her right away. Selective vision. He was escorting Wonder Woman that evening. The music was loud enough to drown out any awkwardness; we steered through small talk. He was standing so close to me that I couldn't see his costume. I said, "Who are you?" He took a step back. Leather jacket, gun holster, whip—he was Indiana Jones.* Didn't turn me on at all (wink). I felt fine until she started intertwining her fingers with his— an act of animated handholding. My stomach did a somersault. I'm pretty sure the rest of me remained standing. Then it was over. He said, "I'm gonna get a drink," and he walked away.

My friend Karina was 180 degrees behind me. As I turned to relay what had happened someone reached out and grabbed me. It was Rollergirl. She was standing on the booth seat in front of me and suddenly her hands were on my shoulders. She said, "I've been wanting to tell you all night that I think you're beautiful." I stared at her in disbelief. What the? Who are you? How is it that you happen to be right here right now with this random yet magical message? Not just, "You look nice" or "I like your costume." Not even, "I think you're beautiful," but it was something she'd been meaning to tell me all night. Her grip on my shoulders gave it a sense of urgency. This was as supernatural an experience as they come.

It could have been anything: maybe she was inebriated, or she enjoys finding fools at parties to give artificial compliments to. I've even thought perhaps Rollergirl picked up on what was happening with the little triangle in front of her—which would

* The only pseudonym not randomly selected

mean perception is her superpower. I'll go with, as I went with that night, it was a genuine moment of female camaraderie. I've done it—gone out of my way to tell a woman how amazing she looks—because, why not. We're all on the same side. Whatever the reason, words could not express my gratitude. I managed a "thank you" and asked, "What is your name?" I wanted to remember her and her impeccable timing forever. It was Bethany (her real name).

While conversation with Indiana went okay, I didn't handle the aftermath well. He caught me looking in his direction. I wondered why he said anything to me at all. In fairness, it would have upset me more if I'd spotted him and he didn't say hello, so there was that. There was no good outcome for me. Then I had a brilliant idea. I could leave. I asked Karina if she minded and she was happy to head to the next club. I was grateful to have a good friend and another party to go to, but the rest of the night wasn't easy. I was reminded of how badly I wanted to be with him and, again, how that just wasn't on my list of options. Not to mention Wonder Woman was about to have the costume sex I craved. Every now and then, though, my woeful thoughts were interrupted and a smile jaywalked across my face when I thought about my girl Rollergirl.

The next day I decided to unfriend Indy. I went to his profile page and scrolled through one last time. A pretty lady named Crystal had posted a message that went something like, "It's been ages. We need to grab drinks soon." A hottie named Jessica said, "I'll be in New York the first week in November. I think you owe me dinner ;)." Yeah it was a good time for me to exit. He was right, he was un-datable. I wanted to be with him; he wanted to run around. I took comfort in knowing his attention was spread out and not honed in on one woman.*

As the year ended I met a man at a holiday party and we started seeing each other. When I was with this man, I was able to give him my undivided attention. When I wasn't, I thought of Indiana. The man I dated was open about not being over his ex-wife, and for that reason I didn't feel we were misleading each other—just enjoying each other's company. We had a nice intellectual chemistry but not so much a sexual one. We dated through the spring and went our separate ways in May.

The weather grew warm and I grew antsy. I was aching to return to my old sexual stomping ground. I tried to forget about Indy—honest I did—but I wanted a weekend. I knew it wouldn't go anywhere, but I wanted marathon sex and mimosas just the same. I e-mailed him—a message friendly and pointless. He would know that saying hello was code for, "Come hither." When he responded the first few lines of his e-mail were as nonchalant as mine, but then he got to the point, "I'm not sure how to put this but I want you to hear from me that I am engaged." Not one who's prone to claustrophobia, the walls came in on me. With Jack I knew he was in a relationship. Here, I knew nothing. I'd done a good job of steering cyber clear, so there was nothing to break my fall. I hit the pavement face first.

Sure, it had occurred to me that he might get married someday, but the un-datable one had made this lifelong commitment in less than a year—since last October (November at

* This is a ri-fucking-diculous thing to take comfort in.

midnight) when he had (count 'em) four women on his roster. If you're an idiot and you know it, clap your hands. I was crushed under the weight of my own foolishness. I cried as I wrote back and said congratulations. I probably didn't owe him one, but I didn't have it in me to be anything but nice to him. I posed one question: "Do you mind if I ask who she is?" It was Wonder Woman. The irony of her costume was not lost on me.

Today, I am so glad this went down the way it did. Fist bump to the universe. Even finding out he had a girlfriend would not have been the backhand across the face that I needed to wake up and figure out how to stop ending up in this situation. I also don't think Indiana and I would have worked well in the long run. At the time, I couldn't love. I could only cling. As for him, I'm not sure the transition from being a man of many women to being man of one is as easy as he made it look. I could be wrong; I often am—especially when this cad is concerned.

In the end, once the shock passed, I was, fortunately, upset with the right person. If you're angry at everyone else nothing will change, if you're angry with yourself you can do something about it. To the altar with him. To the therapist with me.

Now to the most important matter: If your name is Bethany and you were dressed as Rollergirl at a club called Southside on the corner of Broome St. and Cleveland Place on October 31, 2008, find me. Sweetheart, I want to buy you a drink. If, in the ultimate twist of fate, we run into Indiana, I'm going to ask you to make out with me. It will be a nice, dignified make-out session between old friends. I've also considered that you don't exist. You were just an angel passing through—dressed as a porn star on roller skates.

HE SAID HE DIDN'T WANT TO GET MARRIED,
AND THEN DID

It happened in 1989. In the movie *When Harry Met Sally*, Sally laments to Harry, "He just met her . . . She's supposed to be his transitional person, she's not supposed to be the ONE. All this time I thought he didn't want to get married. But, the truth is, he didn't want to marry me." It also happened in 1999 on the last episode of *Sex and the City*, season two. Carrie asks the recently engaged Big "Hey, I have a question for you. Why wasn't it me? I really need to hear you say it." Big's insightful answer, "I don't know." It happened yet again in 2009 with a gender role reversal. In the movie *500 Days of Summer*, Tom Hansen falls madly in love with Summer Finn. Summer happily dates Tom while professing she doesn't believe true love exists. Shortly after they break up, Tom sees her showing off her engagement ring at a party.

Movies can't be trusted regarding special effects, cowboys in space, and perfect lighting during sex, but when emotional interaction is concerned, they speak the truth. Scripts are written by human beings drawing from their own experience to get the job done. Scott Neustadter, cowriter of *500 Days of Summer*, admitted that the film is based on his true story. This clue appears before the opening credits: "The following is a work of fiction. Any resemblance to people living or dead is purely coincidental. Especially you, Jenny Beckman . . . Bitch." My point is the person who says s/he doesn't want to get married and then does is a cliché—as is the well-meaning, deluded soul who believes it.

Before I had my own encounter, I watched this scenario unfold twice with guy friends of mine. Let's call them Brandon and Dylan. Brandon's story first: He was three years into a relationship with Kelly Taylor when she started to mention marriage. Brandon declared, "I don't want to think about marriage until I'm thirty-five." He was thirty-two-ish at the time. Having recently read the book *He's Just Not That Into You*, I suggested to him that maybe he *did* want to get married, just not to Kelly. "That's not it!" he protested fervently. Kelly and Brandon eventually broke up; a year later he was engaged. By the time he was thirty-five he was married with two kids.

I liked Kelly a lot. She and I got along very well, but at the end of the day my loyalties were with Brandon. He could have told me he didn't plan to marry her. I would have kept his secret (although I might have told him I didn't think that was very nice). When he got married I realized what had happened; he'd been lying to himself. After three years, admitting that he didn't want to marry Kelly would mean breaking up with her. He had a demanding job and the thought of entering the dating scene again probably exhausted him. He wanted to keep things as they were without committing further.

Dylan next. He was casually dating a girl named Brenda but kept saying, "I don't want to be in a relationship." I've known this man for a long time, so I know that he prefers monogamy. I told him that he did want to be in a relationship, just not with Brenda. He, like Brandon before him, denied it. He talked to this poor girl on the phone for an hour every day. Not because he was crazy about her, but because his job keeps him in his car for long periods of time and he likes talking to people to make the ride go more quickly. I told him if a man talked to me for an hour every day I'd think he liked me—a lot. Then one day he met Valerie. He called me to say, "You're right. I do want to be in a relationship. What do I do?" He broke it off with Brenda—catching her completely off guard no doubt.

In the end, Valerie broke Dylan's heart. Shortly thereafter he started seeing Donna Martin and began singing his old song: "I don't want to be in a relationship." This time I got frustrated. "Dylan, we've been through this," I said. "You do want to be in a relationship. You're just using this girl." "I am not using her!" he snapped. Mind you, Dylan is not a manipulative person; he doesn't wake up in the morning, rub his hands together and say, "Whose feelings can I hurt today?" But if he were being honest with himself it would go something like, "Look, I know I don't want to be with this girl but if I'm not dating her, then I'm not dating anyone and [whispers] my ego can't handle that." After Donna, he started dating Andrea and eventually married her.

In fairness to the boys, they aren't the only ones in denial. We are too. That's why we believe things like, "I don't want to get married until I'm thirty-five" or "I'm un-datable." It hurts significantly less to believe that than to reconcile the fact that he doesn't want what we want. By believing it, however, we're not avoiding the pain—just delaying it. The day will come when those words can be bought into no more. Having seen this scenario play out twice, I still chose to believe Indiana wouldn't commit to one woman because it gave my feelings some breathing room. However, my focus should've been on the simple fact that he didn't want to be with me; everything after that was a non-issue. The worst part is when you set aside what you want to accommodate the guy; you become a casual chameleon asserting, "Humbug. Who wants to be in a relationship?" When it turns out that he does, you feel like a fool and realize that in order to spend time with him, you abandoned you.

If you want to be exclusive with someone and he gives you the runaround, honor your intentions and walk away (unless your goal isn't to be with the guy but rather to write a song, screenplay, or book. If that's it—you're on the right track). Continue searching for a man who wants what you want. As you walk away, start to make your peace with the fact that the noncommittal guy could be in a relationship this time next week. Again, it's nothing personal (that's next to impossible to believe in this situation, I realize). It has nothing to do with you. When it feels right—for whatever reason—pretty much everyone is willing to commit.

There is also the cab light theory from *Sex and the City*, which says it's more a matter of timing. From season three, episode 8:

CHARLOTTE: Sometimes you just know, it's like, magic, it's fate.

MIRANDA: It's not fate; his light is on, that's all.

CHARLOTTE: What light?

MIRANDA: Men are like cabs, when they're available their light goes on. They awake one day and decide they're ready to settle down, have babies, and they turn their light on. Next woman they pickup, boom, that's the one they'll marry. It's not fate, it's dumb luck.

CHARLOTTE: I'm sorry, I refuse to believe that love is that random.

MIRANDA: Please, it's all about timing. You gotta get 'em
when their light's on.
CARRIE: All the men I meet are flashing yellows.
MIRANDA: Or off duty. They can drive around for years
picking up women and not be available.

This isn't to take away from the women who jump in the
cabs at the right time. I'm sure they're wonderful. But so are
Brenda Walsh, Kelly Taylor, you, and me. In my life thus far, I
have encountered many Indianas and Dylans who are happy to
hang out and hook up but who won't enter a relationship. I
advise you to run in the opposite direction from them. I cannot
speak from personal experience to the Brandon situation. I can
only assume it must be difficult to be in a relationship with a
guy for a few years and listen to him say he doesn't want marriage. Greg Behrendt, coauthor of *He's Just Not That Into You*,
believes this is evidence of the man knowing on some level he
still hasn't found the woman he wants to marry, as explained in
the chapter, "He's Just Not That Into You If He Won't Marry
You." It was true with Brandon and Kelly. On the flip side, I
can name four couples who dated for a decade—with the man
being apathetic about marriage for much of the time—until
one day he opened himself to it. All four couples appear to be
doing well. If you don't want to wait a decade, then you may
want to take your leave—knowing he could be married within
a year. And you could be married the year after that and grateful that the relationship didn't work out after all.

Aside from stinging rejection, part of the reason it hurts to
find out a man you wanted to be with is getting married is

because we assume marriage is what it appears to be. *Looks like eternal happiness from here. Now he has access to it and I don't.* I'll tell you what he has: a lifelong relationship; it's a challenge if ever there was one. It can be a worthwhile challenge or an endless struggle. They don't say, "for better or for worse" just for fun. It can go in either direction, depending on the day. Dylan's marriage did not work out. Brandon's marriage remains strong. He is open about the many roses and occasional thorns that come with family life. Once the initial pain has passed, know that the guy whose last name you really wanted tattooed on your foot experiences joy and sorrow, the same as you do.

> Tom: *You never wanted to be anybody's girlfriend, and now you're somebody's wife.*
> Summer: *It surprised me, too.*
> —From the movie 500 *Days of Summer*, written by
> Scott Neustadter and Michael H. Weber

DON'T DARE TO COMPARE YOURSELF TO HER . . .

There were two main objectives in asking Indiana whom he was marrying. First, genuine curiosity: "I give up. Which one?" The second, predictably, was to make direct comparisons. This is par for the course for me and for the former first lady of South Carolina. In the September 2009 issue of *Vogue*, Jenny Sanford admitted to looking in on her husband's—former South Carolina Governor Mark Sanford—Argentinean mistress. According to the magazine, "Even so, like the rest of America, she and a friend couldn't resist Googling the woman at the center of the firestorm. 'What woman wouldn't want to know what her husband's mistress looks like?' asked the friend. (Sanford's reported verdict: 'She's pretty.')"

My investigation into Wonder Woman began on Facebook, where I encountered the engagement photo that left me blind for three days. *Not going there again. Now what?* I had stayed long enough to get her full name—Diana Prince—so I took my search to LinkedIn. By a show of hands, how many people here have used LinkedIn for professional purposes? Me neither. It is, however, an ideal place for cyber-comparing because you can learn about someone without suffering the sight of intimate photos.

My cousin Kate was sitting next to me as I was doing this devious deed. About Kate: she graduated in the top twenty-five of her class from NYU Medical School; the woman is not too intellectually shabby. I got to Diana's page and told Kate what she does for a living—for anonymity's sake let's say she's a rocket scientist. Kate says, "Oh God. I'm sorry. I'm sorry she's not a trophy wife." This sent the two of us into a laughing fit. It was the perfect response because it made me realize that what I was about to do (i.e., compare myself to Diana) was ridiculous. Don't get me wrong, I have clocked in (too many) hours of my life comparing myself to the other women—notably Jack's wife—and this was a great time to stop because I knew exactly what all that comparing does. Nothing. It doesn't change the situation. As Maya Angelou said of her heartache, "I could not use hate to ease the pain." That's what comparing is—using hate to ease the pain. You're either hating on the other woman (if you believe you're better) or you're hating on yourself (if you believe she's better). Both are unnecessary and counterproductive to the ultimate goal, which is love by way of self-love.

The first paralyzing comparison we seek to make is her looks vs. mine, however, the way a person looks is never the deciding factor in choosing to be in a relationship. Of course appearance can spark the interest, but there needs to be more to it. Can you imagine, "Honey I think you're gorgeous. I don't think you have any other redeeming qualities, but you sure are pretty." If nothing else, two people need to be able to have a conversation—a long one—to move forward. Yet when it comes time to compare ourselves to the new woman in his life we act as if looks are the only consideration. If we think she's more attractive, we sulk, thinking, Of course he picked her. She's stunning. If, in our not-so-humble opinion, we believe we are more attractive, then we throw a temper tantrum: "I don't get it. I just don't get it!" The harsh reality is, his relationship is not for us to get. They have decided to be together for reasons known only to them. Or unknown to them. The decision to marry can be careless—as it was with Jack—but it's still not our concern.

Making critical comparisons doesn't solve the problem. The problem is you're hurt and don't want to be. Comparing is try- ing to walk around the pain, but there is only one way to get to the other side: by walking through it. As you're slogging through the muck, feel free to ask, "What's in this for me?" The answer? Love. Love is in it for you. The day you stop crit- icizing other people is the day you have officially stopped criti- cizing yourself. When you no longer feel the need to compare, it means you've stopped using other people as a litmus test for your own self-worth. This is a challenging feat, and it doesn't happen in a single day. I'm still critical and catch myself doing comparisons now and then, but I do it refreshingly less often than I used to. The Diana Prince situation was a turning point; not comparing myself to her was a major attempt at learning to lift myself up without putting someone else down.

Not criticizing versus being critical is like the difference between doing pull-ups and crushing an anthill under your stiletto. The latter feels better in the short term, but the former feels so much better in the long run. Unless this girl is a friend of yours, she's done nothing wrong. The two of you have the same taste in men and you probably have other things in common as well. I left Diana's LinkedIn page with my curiosity satisfied and knowing I was going to have to move on in a way that didn't involve comparison.

When I spoke of envy earlier, I didn't mention being envious of another woman's intellectual capacity. Intellect, like beauty, is never the deciding factor. It's a contributing factor—as it should be—but we are multidimensional beings. There's more than one trait we possess that will appeal to potential partners. Pulling out one of her dimensions and comparing it to one of yours is like looking at a colorful tile and saying you've seen Sistine Chapel's ceiling. I have the good fortune of being surrounded by brilliant women. You've met my cousin Kate. My cousin Jennifer has her MBA from Harvard. My sister is a CPA and has two master's degrees: an MBA and an MAFM (Masters in Accounting and Financial Management). There's another Jennifer in my life—a good girlfriend—who is a two-time American Women's Chess Champion. I also have friends whose GPAs I know nothing of—nor do I care because they dazzle me with their other talents. I stand proudly among these women because I admire them and because I've got my own thing going on; I've carved out my own creative corner of the universe. No, I don't have an invisible airplane, but I'm not going to lose sleep over it. There's no need to be intimidated by über-intelligent women. They can do things you can't, and you can do things they can't. We are different stars in the same magnificent sky.

...OR TO HIM

While trying not to compare yourself to the woman in his life, maybe also take a stab at not comparing your life situation to his. It's easy to play winners/losers in a circumstance like this. "He's married; he wins," you say to yourself, or "I'm skinnier than his wife therefore I win!" Winning implies that someone has reached the blissful point of no return and that misery is gone—only happy days from here on out. We've talked about this; it doesn't happen. To anyone.

So he got married, moved in with someone, or the like. He wasn't crowned king. Even if he did ascend the throne, he's got a host of bureaucratic frustrations waiting for him. Nothing about marriage or monarchal reign is automatic. They are emotional investments, which means that you have to put a lot in if you want to get anything out. His marriage will be what he and his wife make of it. Your life—including your marriage—will be what you make of it. There are triumphant days ahead for you and there are disappointing days ahead for him and vice versa. Unless you figure out a way to keep day-to-day score (I had 3.7 more marvelous days than he did this year, woohoo!) you're better off sending the concept of winners and losers downstream.

Initially, you'll be devastated, hurt and angry. An old flame's new girlfriend/engagement/marriage will send you into I'll-Show-Him mode. I urge you to go there. Feel everything. And then use that energy to your advantage. Start a new exercise regime. Take up fencing. Join the Peace Corps. Harness your figure skating skills. Be not afraid. Let your creative juices flow like milk and honey. On the other side you'll realize that the only person you had to show anything to was yourself. He gave you reason to doubt yourself, and this is the painful yet worthwhile process of reinstating your self-worth. When this phase ends, start to leave I'll-Show-Him behind and set your sights on Everyone-Is-Fine.

Here's what Everyone-Is-Fine looks like: Justin Timberlake is married. His ex-girlfriend Cameron Diaz is not. I don't worry about Cammy. She's doing great. Girlfriend turned forty, fit as a fiddle, and proclaimed in the November 2012 issue of British *Esquire*, "I know more than I've ever known. I have gratitude. I know myself better. I feel more capable than ever. And as far as the physicality of it—I feel better at 40 than I did at 25." Amen. Justin and Cameron are friendly. They made the movie *Bad Teacher* together. Everyone is fine.

While not married, Lance Armstrong has had two children with girlfriend Anna Hansen since calling off his engagement with singer Sheryl Crow. In that time Sheryl has not gotten married but has adopted two children and entered her fifties like a goddess. Lance, on the other hand, has imploded. Sheryl doesn't have to be glad things didn't work out. I am happy enough for her! The only person here who might not be fine is Lance, but he doesn't know that. He can convince himself of anything. Therefore everyone is fine.

One more example—non-romantic this time. In 2003, Lauren Weisberger got the type of revenge most people only dream of. She wrote a thinly veiled novel about the daily horrors of working for her former boss, *Vogue* editor Anna Wintour. As if the bestselling book wasn't enough, the movie *The Devil Wears Prada* was a critical and commercial hit. Lauren has gone on to write several more successful novels. Meanwhile, back at Condé Nast, Anna Wintour is fine. More than fine—her power in the fashion industry grows at a rate of 57 percent per annum. For a moment in time, Lauren was a fly in the eminent editor's Dom Pérignon. Anna's career didn't miss a beat. If anything, *The Devil Wears Prada* made her more famous. Lauren's star has soared as well; so I doubt she's is waiting for Anna to fall off the Ferris wheel. She probably knows she would only be making herself miserable by doing so.

Anxiously hoping a nuclear meltdown will happen near your ex's house or praying for a severe drought to ruin his crops hurts you more than it hurts him. It's normal at first—anger is part of the grieving process—but letting it go is the final phase of healing. What's in it for you? A heart that is mended, whole and ready to love again—more fully this time. If you find out someday that he's gained some serious sympathetic baby weight or that his wife left him for Fabio, some schadenfreude is also normal. Enjoy but don't linger there too long—bitterness is bad for the complexion. Take a broken heart, agonize over it, make it work for you, and then let it go. If you can't bring yourself to wish him well, the next best place to be is neutral—as in, you don't give a damn. This is a man you once professed to care for deeply. The only entity that can stay angry with him forever is your ego. That's the loser best left by the side of the road.

Isn't it kind of silly to think that tearing someone else down builds you up?

—Sean Covey, *The 7 Habits Of Highly Effective Teens*

SEVEN

UNREQUITED IN A ROOM FULL OF REQUITEDS

Why can't you just be happy for me and then go home and talk
about me behind my back like a normal person?!

—From the movie *Bridesmaids*, written by

Kristen Wiig and Annie Mumolo

I've alluded to it, and now I'm going to say it: single people have the same capacity for happiness that couples do, and couples have the same capacity for unhappiness that single people do. Relationship status does not denote overall life fulfillment. Attached or unattached—each individual is responsible for the state of his or her own well-being. The same is true of having or not having children. Couples without children can access the same set of emotions that couples with children can—couples with children taking in a bit more stress? Perhaps. Why do I point all of this out? Because from what I've seen, many people appear to have no idea this is the case. Plenty of single people are miserable and they blame it on being single, while some married folk are unsatisfied and blame it on their partner, their children, or their lack of children. As long as we have a person or situation to blame our discontent on, we can keep from realizing that we (me, myself, and I) are in charge of our own internal satisfaction.

I know it's hard to believe that couples haven't cornered the market on happiness (and I say that without irony). It's generally assumed otherwise because there is one thing that couples have that single people do not—and it's a big thing. It's something many people equate with happiness: normalcy. According to societal standards, it's 100 percent more normal to be part of a couple than it is to be alone. To be attached is to not have people whispering and wondering what your problem is. For some, this is reason enough to stay in a relationship even if the relationship is low quality. The fear of nonconformity is a subset of the fear of being alone, as described by my BFF Erich Fromm: "If I am like everybody else, if I have no feelings or thoughts which make me different, if I conform to the custom, dress, ideas, to the pattern of the group, I am saved; saved from the frightening experience of aloneness."

We are a society that values outward proof more than inward gratification. Another person by your side is evidence—sometimes even to you—that you are desirable. It can be difficult to attend a wedding alone, although I imagine it can also be difficult to attend a wedding if there's turbulence in your relationship. But no one need know what's going on with the couple—they can hide behind each other. They can also make a scene. A few years ago, I was a single bridesmaid at a wedding. I had a blast. One of my fellow married bridesmaids fought audibly with her husband throughout the reception.

There are as many examples of bitter singles, couples, and
parents as there are of blissful singles, couples, and parents.
The point isn't to play tit for tat, but to recognize that the emotional playing field is level. Actively believing that happiness
exists over there but not here is what keeps us perpetually longing for a different life. If, as a single person, you play "Things
will be better when . . ." you'll play that game as part of a couple
also. "Things will be better when . . . we're married . . . but
then other couples seem happier than we are . . . let's have
kids . . . more kids . . . oh look, don't the couples without kids
have a lot of freedom . . . things will be better when our kids go
to school . . ."

Like all fear, the fear of nonconformity lends itself to bad
decision making. According to research conducted by Jennifer
Gauvain, a licensed clinical social worker and coauthor of *How
Not to Marry the Wrong Guy: Is He "the One" or Should You
Run?: A Guide to Living Happily Ever After*, 30 percent of now-
divorced women say they knew they were making a mistake
on their wedding day, and they went ahead anyway. Based on
Gauvain's investigation these are the most common reasons
why:

1. We've dated for so long, I don't want to waste all the
   time we have invested in the relationship.
2. I don't want to be alone.
3. He'll change after we get married.
4. It is too late, too embarrassing, and/or too expensive to
   call off the wedding.
5. He is a really nice guy; I don't want to hurt his feelings.

There is fear and denial behind each of these reasons—the fear of nonconformity among them. Conformity, while a relief at first, can be dangerous. It's what's behind a midlife crisis—waking up one day and realizing you did everything you were "supposed" to do but not anything you wanted to do. Your imaginative self wonders, "Why have I been ignored all this time?" As the axiom goes, you're more likely to regret the things you didn't do rather than the things you did.

In this way, unrequited love can be, strangely again, an asset. Having relationships not work out forces you to be a non-conformist. You have to make your way through social gatherings of all kinds with people asking "Anyone new in your life?" You seek and find your people—other singles who are going through what you're going through—and you figure out how to navigate the couple consortium, making all kinds of interesting observations along the way. You separate the wheat couples—those who love and accept you as you are—from the chaff couples—those who condescend and subtly suggest "But don't you want what I have?" Like the fear of being alone, if you conquer the fear of nonconformity, you are equipped to make the most of life no matter the circumstances. And, once more, if and when you enter a relationship it's because you want to, not because you're afraid not to.

Conformity aside, I know what it's like to want to make a carnal connection with another human being. The desire to discover and be discovered intellectually and sexually is as authentic a yearning as can be. It's not that I don't want it (very much); rather, I've accepted that I cannot force it. I cannot force the men I feel for to feel for me. Nor can I force myself to feel romantically for the men who express an interest in me. I've attempted both to devastating results. Looking back, I wonder why I would ever want to force such a thing anyway. Now I try to meet the universe in the middle. I am in charge of my own destiny to a certain extent and I put forth an honest effort, personally and professionally, to the degree I can. When things don't work out I rely on Miss Universe (the all-knowing one, not the pageant one) to have a reason—whether she shares it with me or not. I seek solace in the present moment; try to focus on what I have rather than what I lack; and trust love's timing.

Looking for love while in the company of couples who appear to have it can be difficult. Know that some of them have it—absolutely—while others are putting on a show. Keep in mind that those who have it don't have it every single second of the day. Love ebbs and flows. There are peaks and valleys; yins and yangs. Remember that each member of a couple is human; they feel everything you feel: embarrassment, amusement, nausea, insecurity, delight, and even—wait for it—loneliness. I have it on the good authority of several women married for thirty-plus years that it's completely possible to feel isolated and disconnected from the person sharing the same bed. Loneliness is a frame of mind; it has little to do with how many people are in the room.

Wanting to be in a relationship and have a family are noble aspirations depending on your reason. I encourage you to think past, "It's what you're supposed to do," and "It will make me happy." In *The Mastery of Love*, Don Miguel Ruiz declares, "Relationship is an art. The dream two people create is more difficult to master than one." This makes sense, doesn't it? That it's more challenging to deal with two sets of problems

rather than just one—more than two if you have children. I'm
not suggesting you avoid it because it's a challenge—the opposite in fact. Go to it because it is a challenge. The problem is,
many people don't see romantic relationships as a challenge but
rather the solution to life's problems. I follow Alisa Bowman,
author of *Project: Happily Ever After: Saving Your Marriage
When the Fairytale Falters*, on Twitter. She's posted this amusing maxim more than once: "A spouse is someone who will
stand by you through all of the problems you wouldn't have
had if you stayed single." The only problem you solve by being
in a relationship is the problem of being single. If you view
being single as a problem, it will go away and new problems
will appear in its place.

We have, therefore, established in our culture that being
coupled up is normal and being single is not. But how much
faith should we put in normalcy? How about we call it the
Loch Ness Monster of social concepts—in other words, believing in it is optional. Believe in it and then relish in being a rebel
for a while. Also know that your friends in relationships might
need you and your independence someday. One of my cousins
is readying her spare room for a recently divorced friend. The
blushing bride of yesterday might be the disillusioned wife of
today. Last year's single girl is this year's mother. Our outward
situations are in constant motion; accepting that harmony is
available to us no matter the external circumstance is one way
to steady yourself on the inside. This way, love of self and love
of life remain constant through it all.

*Most people are not even aware of their need to conform. They
live under the illusion that they follow their own ideas and incli-*

nations, that they are individuals, that they have arrived at their
opinions as the result of their own thinking—and that it just hap-
pens that their ideas are the same as those of the majority.

—Erich Fromm, *The Art of Loving*

ANSWERING QUESTIONS ABOUT
YOUR RELATIONSHIP STATUS

I think it's important to bring up every single person's favorite
question: "Are you seeing anyone?" But I must confess that I
feel underqualified to address it, because I'm still figuring out a
way to handle it myself. For the longest time I thought this
question made me uncomfortable because I had the wrong answer—but now I think the question itself is faulty. It implies
that there is a right answer and that you're behind the curve if
your answer is no.

At my mother's sixtieth birthday party a friend of hers
asked me, "Is there anyone special in your life?" and I replied,
"There are lots of special people in my life." Instead of letting
me avoid the question, as I was trying to do with a smile, she
felt the need to clarify: "No, what I mean is: Are you dating
anyone?" We both felt the awkwardness as I said no. She's a
warm, wonderful woman and I know she meant no harm.
Many people are holding a social script of what everyone's
life—including their own—should look like by a certain age,
and it doesn't register when someone seems to have missed
her cue.

There was a time in my life when I would answer the question "Are you seeing anyone?" quickly and with a qualifica-
tion: "No . . . but I will. I mean, I keep meaning to set up an

online profile." I shudder when I recall my reactions. I have
since had *the talk* with myself: "You don't owe anyone an expla-
nation or apology for who you are and how you live your life. A
simple 'no' will do if it's the truth." Or will it? On more than
one occasion, my no has been met with, "Don't you think if you
did [insert list of suggestions that imply I am an error that must
be corrected] you'd have more luck?" Interestingly, it's not just
couples that ask. I have one gregarious gal pal who shouts, "Are
you dating anyone?" at me oftentimes before she says hello. She
asks me because the answer for her is always yes. She is a pro-
lific online dater, and that's fine with me. It's her method. It's
not mine.

When people offer me suggestions on how I can fix the
problem of being single, it's because they see it as a problem.
They can't imagine themselves in my position, so they try to
rescue me, not considering that I don't mind being here. If I
have to choose between dating someone I'm not interested in
for the sake of pleasing the peanut gallery and being single, I
choose the latter. Don't get me wrong, I'd swim across the
ocean for a man I wanted to be with, but in the interim the
only time being single bothers me is when someone asks me if
I'm seeing anyone. Whenever I'm asked that, all I hear is,
"When are you going to be normal?" The fact that that's how
I interpret the question is, admittedly, my problem—it seems
that part of my subconscious is still holding on to the script,
too. Ideally, the day will come when I have the sharpest set of
not-taking-it-personally knives there is and can answer as non-
chalantly as if I were replying to, "What time is it?"

Recently a girlfriend of mine declared, "The next time
someone asks me if I'm seeing anyone I'm going to say, 'No.

Are you having any trouble in your relationship?' Because it's the same question. It is an equally personal question!" She and I laugh about it but have to yet to muster the courage to reply that way. She makes a good point, though. My friends have relationship troubles that I never have to ask about because they tell me. If they want to talk to about it, they will. The same way if I'm seeing someone new, I will offer it up to the gods of conversation. I try to be mindful of this and refrain from asking other people questions that imply they are incomplete. For example: When are you two getting married? When do you plan to have children? When are you going to have *another* child? I strive to enjoy life in this moment and try not to rush myself—or anyone else—to the next stage.

Over drinks one night my friend Dana asked if I was seeing anyone, and when I answered no she straightened herself in frustration and said, "Oh my God. I know so many great girls who aren't dating right now!" That comment frightened away any discomfort that dared to linger, and it brought me back to earth. Of course that's why they ask, because they're my friends and they want good things for me. It's important for me to remember that, but it's also important for me to assert that I'm okay. When your friends tell you how magnificent you are, it's easy to go into pity mode: "My friends think I'm great—why haven't I met anyone?" Naturally, your friends think you're wonderful; that's why they're your friends. However, they have limited jurisdiction over your destiny; and vice versa. It doesn't matter how qualified I believe a friend is for a job—I can't give it to him. It doesn't matter how wonderful of a mother I believe a friend will make—I can't make her fertility issues go away. Sitting around the campfire listening to your friends say, "But you're so smart and pretty, and we just don't get it" is focusing on what's perceived as missing. I say reroute—don't encourage conversation that suggests you're incomplete. An incomplete person takes her identity and purpose from others. A complete person gives; she gives love and empathy to those in her life now and is better equipped to someday give love to her significant other and, if she chooses to become a mother, her children.

There was one especially interesting evening when my answer to the dating question was, "Yes, I am seeing someone," and it still wasn't right—according to my dinner party. A few Memorial Day Weekends ago I was being courted by a new guy and introduced him to my friends—two couples—on a Friday night. Saturday night we got together again, but my man couldn't make it and I went alone. A detail that needs to be shared is that the four people I was at the restaurant table with were high. I have no problem with that—it was a holiday weekend and they were relaxing—but it's not a pardon. I don't believe that drugs and alcohol make you an entirely different person—they simply knock down the wall of social protocol. In other words, this is what we would say if there were no rules. I was unsuspectingly criticized by two people—the other two were far gone.

The first attack question was, "So, four months, huh?" implying that my relationship shouldn't have even gotten to that point. She continued to ask patronizing questions, which I naively tried to answer—having yet to pick up on what was happening. It's generally not my first assumption that people I've known for years are making fun of me. She would then interrupt me with, "You know this isn't going to work!" Somewhere in the middle of the interrogation, I looked across the table and the guy—a friend of six years—was mocking the man I was dating, mimicking his mannerisms and his voice. What upsets me the most is that I didn't leave. I said good night to them politely and it took a few more hours for what had happened to sink it. It was the last time I saw that guy friend. This was in May and he e-mailed me an apology sometime after Labor Day. Patching things up wasn't a priority to him even when he recovered his mental faculties. It's unusual for a friendship to end on the spot like that, but when true colors turn out to be varying shades of condescending and inconsiderate, there's nothing else to do.

On another night—in a galaxy far from that one—I went to another dinner, one that was equally memorable for the exact opposite reason. I was at Carnegie Hall at the invitation of my good friend Patrick, who's on the Board of Trustees of the New York Youth Symphony. He'd invited me to their Christmas concert and afterward there was a reception dinner. I was mingling around the bar when I met Rachel. We introduced ourselves and I asked what brought her to the show that night. As it turned out, her husband, Matt, had just gotten off stage conducting a jazz band. I repeat: Her husband had just gotten off stage conducting a jazz band at Carnegie Hall. Is that what she wanted to discuss? Not really. She wanted to talk about me and find out who I was. When she found out I was writer, she was overjoyed. Matt came over and she excitedly introduced me, saying, "This is Samara. She's a writer." They were sincere and delightful. For the rest of the night, our conversation went like this: "Let's talk about you." "No, let's talk about *you*." "No, you." "No, really, you." They didn't ask if I was seeing anyone, and I didn't ask when they were having children, because our lives were rich, complete, and interesting enough in that moment.

Couples that are happy with their lives are not going to piss all over yours. People in general who are satisfied with their lives are not going to come down on you with an avalanche of criticism. Remember: what people say and do tells you what's going on inside them, not what's happening with you. I try to remind myself of this, too, when I'm feeling especially critical—knowing that the most productive way to deal with it is to march over to the mirror and ask, "What's your problem?"

The question "Are you seeing anyone?" will continue to be asked in passing and it's in my best interest to answer without assuming I know where it's coming from—it could be curiosity, concern, or even criticism. If the follow-up to the question, however, starts to veer off into How-Can-We-Fix-You territory it's my job not to let it go there. If others want to stress out over my relationship status, they are welcome. I prefer to remain calm and well rested.

ON BEING HAPPY FOR OTHERS

In early May 2010, I walked into the Madison Hotel in Washington, DC, and went to the front desk to check in. The receptionist said, "Miss O'Shea, you'll be staying with us . . ." and looked at me quizzically, "for twenty-one days?" The answer was yes, and I was the first from my office to arrive. I was working as a legal assistant, and we were in town for trial.

I knew there was a lot of work ahead, but I was excited about this trip. I was looking forward to the overtime pay, the break from routine, and the hotel itself, which was a nice place to stay—it happened to have hosted every president since Kennedy. I was glad to have someone else make my king-size bed and bring me room service while I was hard at work. As the other paralegals and assistants trickled in, we started to set up the war room—the conference room we'd be working out of—before the attorneys arrived. One of my fellow assistants, Grace, came in with an announcement: her boyfriend had proposed over the weekend. Will, our fearless paralegal leader, jumped for joy as only a truly fabulous gay man can. I said congratulations, admired the ring and thought, Are you fucking kidding me? Now I have to listen to her squeal with delight and plan her wedding for the next three weeks. Shoot me.

I knew everyone on the trial support staff team only in passing, and I was nervous about this because they knew each other well. I figured we'd be fine because, you know, we're not teenagers, but part of me was aware that I was the outsider. That all changed as soon as the war room was set up and we went out to lunch. It was the first of many group indulgences that we weren't paying for. At one point during lunch, Will looked at Grace and said, "I'm so happy for you, G. I think you'll be such a good wife and mother." She replied, "Thanks, Will. That's nice of you to say. I always had trouble picking a major in college because I just wanted to be a mom." It was such a sweet, out-of-nowhere exchange, and it softened me. He appeared to be sincerely happy for her and I thought, I want to be able to do that.

We worked twelve-to-eighteen-hour days and I liked the intensity of it. I wouldn't want to work that way forever, but I romanticized it and imagined I was working in a 1970s news-room (*The Washington Post* office was right down the street).

Had it been the 1970s, however, there would have been more social restrictions placed on us all. Our entourage included six: two gay men—both in relationships but not with each other—one single heterosexual (admittedly metrosexual) man, and three hetero women—two single and one recently engaged. Forty years earlier, the gay men may have felt it necessary to keep their orientation quiet and the rest of us would have most likely married right out of college. Instead we had different lifestyles and still shared so much in common. The trip was an active lesson in live and let live.

Being happy for others can be a monumental task—especially when they have something you want. Our instinct to be threatened by someone else's happiness is interesting. Someone shares good news, and we put on a smile while grinding our teeth. We act as if there's a limited supply of happiness and the other person is hoarding it, but I think this is the wrong way to look at it. There's an infinite amount of happiness; more than enough to go around. How does Grace getting engaged in any way hinder me from finding love? It doesn't, yet I interpreted the fact that she found it first as meaning that she was better than I am or that she won.

Contrary to my initial assumption, Grace neither squealed nor started her wedding plans while we were in DC. Instead we had late-night/very-early-morning girl talks. She told me about how some of her fiancé's friends cast her aside because she's younger than he is. She spoke of the relationship troubles they had leading up the engagement. It was all very human. It can be so easy to forget that other people's lives aren't flawless. Having trouble being happy for others is another one of those things that we all go through—not just single women hearing about their friends getting married. It's also couples having trouble getting pregnant hearing about others who do it with ease. People job searching hearing about a friend's promotion. There are countless examples of what someone else could have that might upset you. The thing is, you'll flip-flop back and forth with your friends on this for the rest of your lives. Some days it's you having trouble extending happiness to them while other days it's them struggling to give it to you. Perhaps your career will peak and it might cause your stay-at-home-mom friend to long for her working days. Remember that you are being asked to be happy for a friend in this moment. You will be asked to grieve with a friend in another moment, and your friends will be called upon to do the same for you.

Since we all know what it can feel like to learn of a friend's milestone moment, there's a general empathy passed around. A friend of mine was nervous to tell another friend of ours that she was engaged because it was that friend's mission in life to get married. I was at a baby shower and the mother-to-be told me a cousin of hers had recently had a miscarriage. My friend told her cousin she *completely* understood if she didn't want to come to the shower. She came anyway. It was a beautiful act of bravery. The moments where we can be authentically happy for others are extraordinary because it means that all is well within us—and it signifies love and loyalty to our friends. Some days it's more difficult than others. Be kind to yourself during the more trying times. Treat yourself to a massage on the way home.

If you're not up for being happy for others, I encourage you to stay far away from Facebook. There's nothing but shiny, happy people there. Your friends won't post the photos of the huge argument they had in the car on their way to the airport before flying to paradise. Just paradise—those are the only photos you'll see. You're comparing your life to a microscopic piece of their puzzle.

Back in our nation's capital, we won the case. On our celebratory night out in DC, Grace's husband-to-be drove down and surprised her. I was genuinely happy for her, and I was happy for me, too; by then I had a great new girlfriend and we were doing tequila shots out of champagne flutes. One of the assistants on our co-counsel team made a pass at our resident metrosexual, assuring him that she's in a *very* open marriage. We saw the gamut of relationships that night—the newbies and those who'd been at it for a while. Live and let live.

The individual has always had to struggle to keep from being overwhelmed by the tribe. If you try it, you will be lonely often, and sometimes frightened. But no price is too high to pay for the privilege of owning yourself.

—Friedrick Nietzsche

GREAT EXPECTATIONS

A few years ago I sat down to brunch with a friend. I was in town for her baby shower and this was the first chance she and I had had to catch up without her husband nearby. Just before the food arrived, she volunteered, "So . . . marriage isn't all it's cracked up to be." She went on about some of the struggles they were having while I listened attentively and offered support where I could. There was no schadenfreude on my part; I was too busy being blown away by her honesty. I find people open up over time about how marriage has let them down, but she was still standing on the sacred ground of the first year. I was surprised that she had admitted these things even to herself. I think it was mainly that her disappointment had caught her off guard.

Of course I decided to take this piece of information and be annoying with it the next time I was at my parent's house. I said, "Hey Dad, Mary says marriage isn't all it's cracked up to be." My father looked at me deadpan and said, "What did she expect?" A seemingly cold reply might just be the key to my parent's marriage—solid and amusing at the thirty-five-year mark. More on their marriage in a bit. First, the question: What did she expect? It's an essential question and one we rarely ask ourselves. We're chasing after this thing, but we can't quite put our finger on it. Is it a tax break? Good, you'll get one. Are you hoping to be like everybody else? You'll most likely get that, too—unless you *and* your man are a little off kilter. Do you expect cotton candy every day? That I can't promise. I'm guessing if someone gave you a cotton candy machine as a wedding gift that it would most likely sit in the garage. I doubt my friend Mary thought specifically about what she expected from marriage; she just thought life would be better, in general—as she'd been told.

One reason we expect so much from the future and are regularly let down lies in a theory called hedonic adaptation (also known as the hedonic treadmill). Hedonic adaptation is the innate ability to return to a base level of happiness despite major life changes. The studies of Richard E. Lucas, Ph.D., mentioned in Chapter Two, found that people who win the lottery, after a period of enhanced emotion, find themselves about as happy as the average person. In other words, we adjust easily. What is stimulating this Christmas is commonplace by next Thanksgiving. When we adapt—to people, places, and material goods—we want more, better, different. A new gadget, new dress, new lover can thrill for only so long before we start to take them for granted. Regardless of the external satisfaction that comes our way, we will ultimately return to home base, whether it's perpetual content or perpetual discontent.

Hedonic adaptation combined with our propensity to keep up with the Joneses is a recipe for discontent. A million-dollar salary is great until you buy a house next to people who make five million. Your marriage is sound until Mrs. Robinson stops by to welcome you to the neighborhood. What the bylaws of hedonic adaptation say about romantic relationships is that, after a while, the idea that life might just be better with someone else becomes a tempting thought.

The antidote to the expectation treadmill: learn to love life as it is now. Whatever your circumstance may be—don't expect the pool boy or a bonus check to save you. If you can't find happiness—because your state of affairs doesn't lend to it— seek contentment; stillness in the storm. This doesn't mean don't go after the things you want. But remember that personal challenges—those experiences that satisfy us on the inside— are where we find the most fulfillment. If you don't like your base level, address it within rather than continuing to expect emotional salvation from all things without.

I can tell you exactly what a marriage with reasonable expectations looks like after three decades. As empty nesters of twelve years, my parents have it down. They laugh often, sing silly (read: ridiculous, made up) songs, and make the most of unpredictable situations. I called them during Hurricane Sandy—they were out of power and playing Scrabble by candlelight. There are no secrets in this relationship. If I tell my mother, known to gossip occasionally, "Don't tell anyone," she'll meekly ask, "Can I tell your father?" Recently they've been shopping for a new home and looked at one that apparently had a stunning marble kitchen. The kitchen, however, was closed off—it lacked an open space connecting it with any other room. My father ruled it out immediately. Why? "If I'm in the kitchen cooking and your mother is in the living room reading or working, then we can't talk. We have so many of our conversations that way." That house was stricken from the list because my father would miss my mother too much if there were a wall between the kitchen and the living room. My parents will be the first to tell you that marriage is difficult and there are plenty of days when both parties want out, but they will also tell you that soldiering through those days is well worth it.

Now back to our question: What do you expect? If you're anything like me, what you're expecting/hoping for in the pursuit of romance is just that—romance. I want the newness of love. The quixotic whirl where everything he says is fascinating. It's like talking to Galileo while gazing upon Hugh Jackman. Initiating sex requires no more than a passing glance. It's difficult to imagine he'll ever do anything to annoy me or that we'll even have a disagreement. If we do argue, it's nothing that a passing glance can't cure. Essentially, what I'm after is the dopamine binge that typically lasts twenty-four months. I know—logically, I know—that period is temporary, but it's still an initiation phase I'd like to indulge in fully. Should that happen, what comes next? Hedonic adaptation declares that when passion wanes, one might start to think this partner might not have been the right one after all.

I wonder if disenchantment awaits me, since so much of what I crave is in those glorious early days. As a frame of reference for what life might be like once the infatuation phase is complete, I'll use this moment. I do not have romance (new or old) in my life as I type. It's early evening and I'm in my favorite yoga pants, which means all is well with the world. I'm at ease and switching between the glass of wine, the glass of water, and the cup of tea in front of me. I like to mix it up. Days ago I finished the second semester of a master's degree program. It was highly stressful at times, but the sense of accomplishment is significant—nothing I have ever experienced with school before. A strange thing happens with each assignment. I think, *I can't do this*. That is my knee-jerk reaction to every paper, presentation, and exam and, somehow, I do it—so far I've done it with As. Yet my subconscious insists on climbing the mini-mountain every time.

My social life has been limited for the past few months. There haven't been many photos posted on Facebook and certainly none that would make others envious of my life. Still, I have felt nothing but love and support from my family and friends cheering me on and saying, "See you when you're finished!" In order to write this book, I've had to revisit times when I was inundated with negative emotions. I can see that even in my worst moments, I've never felt hopeless—down but never out. Conclusion: If romance enters my life, takes me on a roller-coaster ride, and drops me (us) off back here—to the way I feel right now—I will not be disappointed at all.

UNTYING THE KNOT

I would like to be clear that I have no issue with marriage. As mentioned, I am the offspring of a couple I put on a pedestal. When I look at them I often think, "This is how you do it." I am the beneficiary of their union, and I know how fortunate I am to be able to say this. When marriage works, it works well and if the opportunity presents itself, mazel tov. My issue lies in the conformity factor—the invisible social pressure that causes some people to mindlessly marry because it's what everyone else is doing and creates suffering as a result. Singles suffer because they aren't with the in crowd and couples that robotically marry suffer because they are caught off guard by the reality of the undertaking. Naturally, not everyone falls into these categories, but enough do to raise an eyebrow.

I propose we end the suffering—especially the self-suffering. Most of the criticism we receive is coming at us from our own heads; we wonder, "Why am I not coupled yet?" What I suggest is that we untie the knot—the one that's been choking us. The one that asphyxiates like this: "My life must absolutely, undoubtedly look like this picture I drew when I was in sixth grade; otherwise I'll be worthless. Things MUST happen in exactly this way at exactly this time or else there'll be hell to pay." There will be hell to pay, all right, but the one to pay it will be you. To insist on a certain outcome—*one* outcome—is to deny yourself the surprise experiences life was going to give you—the things you didn't know you wanted until they came knocking and you were daring enough to let them in. By tying yourself to an ending, you're making arrangements to be miserable if you don't get exactly what you want. Or worse, you get exactly what you want and it doesn't make you as supremely happy as you thought it was going to.

I've spent the last few years untying myself from the *musts*, and it's been fun. Would I like to have a thirty-five-year marriage that looks like my parents'? I sure would. Will I meet that man at a time that works for both of us? I have no idea. I look for love and sometimes love means marriage while other times it means being George Clooney's girlfriend for two years. I can see myself breezing into my early forties unmarried and taking names like Miss Diaz. I've got this hankering lately to live abroad. The two people I admire most on Facebook right now are former colleagues of mine—both single girls—one living in Geneva, Switzerland, and the other in Hong Kong. I believe that life is long and we needn't try to fit ourselves into one idea of what it should look like.

Untying yourself from the way things *have* to be is untying yourself from fear. Fuck fear. Come with me. We're going for a walk. We don't have to stay too long, but I want to show you something. We're going to see the worst-case scenario: the unmarried life. "What's that?" you ask. "Unmarried life? Excuse me, I have this thing . . ." Hold on a minute. Don't go. Just look at it—really quick—from the other side. This is an exercise in perspective, the purpose of which is to remove every fear factor. Let's confront the monster in the closet, so we don't have to be afraid of him anymore. It will be strange at first, but keep walking—go out on the tight rope—and don't look down. What kind of a lame, unadventurous, unsexy, unmemorable life awaits the unwed? Well, without marriage, one might be doomed to end up like these people:

THE FASHION DESIGNER. Gabrielle "Coco" Bonheur Chanel (1883–1971) had hoped to spend her life on the stage as a singer and dancer. Instead, it was her side job as a seamstress that brought her fortune and fame. She liberated women of the early twentieth century from suffocating corsets and offered them the choice of stylish, comfortable clothing—most notably the Chanel suit and the little black dress, which she is oft credited with conceiving. She had lovers—usually wealthy, prominent, and sometimes married men. One of her loves, Captain Arthur Edward "Boy" Capel, financed her first shops in Paris. At the age of forty, Coco began a ten-year relationship with the Duke of Westminster. They did not marry, and she explained why: "There have been several Duchesses of Westminster. There is only one Chanel." She spent the last thirty years of her life living in the Hotel Ritz in Paris. There was no retirement for Coco; the day before she died at age eighty-seven, she was working on the spring catalog. Coco Chanel was the only fashion designer named on *Time* magazine's list of the "Most Influential People of the 20th Century."

THE BASKETBALL LEGEND. As a young man, Wilton Norman "Wilt" Chamberlain (1936–1999) preferred track and field to basketball. He called the latter a "game for sissies," but the culture in his hometown of Philadelphia was one where basketball ruled and he eventually gave in—that and he was 6'11" when he entered high school. Topping off at 7'1", he went on to play for the Harlem Globetrotters, Philadelphia 76ers, and the Los Angeles Lakers. To this day, he is the only NBA player to score one hundred points in a single game.

There were many women in his life—he claimed to have slept with twenty thousand of them—but little romance. He openly admitted that he never came close to marrying and didn't want to have children. Twenty thousand or not, I'm sure the number was high. I tip my hat to the man for his self-awareness. If you know you don't have it in you to be faithful, why pretend?

THE FINANCIER. Theodore Joseph "Ted" Forstmann (1940–2011) was a private equity pioneer and philanthropist. He made a lot of money and gave hundreds of millions of it away to charity. In 1999 he cofounded the Children's Scholarship Fund, which offers scholarships to underprivileged children so they could attend private schools using vouchers—donating fifty million out of his own pocket. He went on to do something not too many single men do—adopt. He met his two sons, Everest and Siya, at an orphanage in South Africa, after having been invited to the country by Nelson Mandela. He gave a million dollars to the orphanage while in town. In addition to philanthropic endeavors, he had an active social life. As an international playboy, he dated Princess Diana, Elizabeth Hurley, and Padma Lakshmi, former model and host of "Top Chef," yet he didn't care to settle down. In 1995 he told *The Washington Post*: "I find the prospect of being married more difficult than most people. I would be a difficult husband." Again, points for self-awareness. Many people get married thinking about what they're getting—not what they're giving. Ted Forstmann looked at the perceived list of requirements to be a good husband and simply didn't see himself.

THE ACTOR. Alfredo James "Al" Pacino (b. 1940). You don't need me to say any more than that, do you? *The Godfather. Scarface. The Devil's Advocate.* Academy Award Winning Best Actor for *Scent of a Woman.* One of my favorite Pacino roles is when he played Dr. Jack Kevorkian in HBO's *You Don't Know Jack.* Al is the only one on this list who has biological children. He had his oldest daughter, born in 1989, with former acting coach Jan Tarrant, and he and actress Beverly D'Angelo had twins in 2001. He is no longer romantically involved with either woman. He continues to act and be a bachelor.

JANE OF ALL TRADES. As an actress, writer, director, producer, real-estate developer, and L'Oréal spokesperson, is there anything Diane Keaton (b. 1946) hasn't done? Get married. She famously had long-term relationships with Woody Allen and Warren Beatty. She also had an on-again, off-again relationship with fellow unmarried thespian Al Pacino during the making of *The Godfather* films. In 1996 she adopted her first son, Dexter, and adopted another boy, Duke, in 2001. She refers to motherhood as, "the most completely humbling experience I've ever had." Keaton publicly opposes plastic surgery and became the face of L'Oréal at the sexy age of sixty. She remains friends with exes Warren and Woody, and has no regrets. Her thoughts on being a spinster: "I don't think that because I'm not married it's made my life any less. That old maid myth is garbage."

THE SECRETARY OF STATE. One Mother's Day, I caught a clip of Condoleezza Rice (b. 1954) on CNN telling a story about her own mother. As a little girl in Alabama, her mother took her to buy an Easter dress. The sales lady told them that she would have to try the dress on in the supply closet, to which her mother replied, "She tries the dress on in the dressing room or we don't buy it." Being born in the segregated South and going on to become the first female African American Secretary of State is an extraordinary journey. In addition to her career in politics, Condoleezza is also an accomplished pianist and has performed publicly with cellist Yo-Yo Ma and singer Aretha Franklin. In the 1970s, Condoleezza was engaged to American football player Rick Upchurch. She ended the relationship because, according to the biography *Twice as Good: Condoleezza Rice and Her Path to Power*, by Marcus Mabry, "She knew the relationship wasn't going to work." Anne Milford and Jennifer Gauvain, coauthors of the book *How Not to Marry the Wrong Guy*, would be proud.

THE COMEDIAN. What would election season be like without Bill Maher (b. 1956)? What would HBO be without him? Not worth paying for. The outspoken satirist ranks number thirty-eight on Comedy Central's one hundred greatest stand-up comedians of all time. He's written seven books and has been sitting at the helm of *Real Time with Bill Maher* since 2003. In the past decade, he's dated a Playboy Cyber Girl (I'm guessing that's a centerfold—just online) and a former hip-hop model, but he openly enjoys his bachelor status. His website quotes him as saying, "I'm the last of my guy friends to have never gotten married, and their wives—they don't want them playing with me. I'm like the escaped slave—I bring news of freedom."

THE SINGER. I already mentioned Sheryl Crow (b. 1962), so I'll just do a quick summary. Sheryl by the numbers: Seven studio albums. Fifty million records sold worldwide. Nine Grammys. Early fifties and fabulous. Two adopted boys. A breast cancer survivor. Ninety-nine problems and Lance Armstrong ain't one.

THE BOMBSHELL. I clearly feel a kinship with Cameron Diaz (b. 1972). We're both tall and unmarried. I sang her praises earlier, so I won't go into too much detail. I'll just say she could still get married—she's only forty-one—but she unapologetically crossed the spinster line. It was noticed and appreciated.

HONORABLE MENTION

THE STAGE SENSATION. My senior year of high school, I was in theater class and there was some Broadway magazine splayed out on one of the desks. My teacher said, "Look at her," pointing to Bernadette Peters (b. 1948), "she's about to turn fifty and her skin looks amazing. Do you know why? She stays out of the sun." Sold! I was an instant convert. I had been to the tanning salon a few times at that point, but that comment ended it for me and it was SPF 45 from then on. That exchange also tuned me into Bernadette herself. She's a sometime movie actress—known for her roles in the Steve Martin classic *The Jerk* and *Annie*—but mostly a stage actress, having been nominated for seven Tony's, winning two. I learned about her love life backward; I heard of the tragic death of her husband and wanted to know more. Looking

into it, I discovered that Bernadette Peters got married for the
first time at the socially unacceptable age of forty-eight to a
man fourteen years her junior—thirty-four-year-old invest-
ment adviser Michael Wittenberg. Google them, they were
adorable, and you can't tell there's an age difference. They
were married for a little over nine years when Michael died in
a helicopter crash in Montenegro. Unimaginably devastating.
Since then the reigning queen of Broadway has triumphed
onstage many times over, done charity work on behalf of animals, and written two children's books. In 2012 she announced
that her late husband was being honored by having a wing
named after him at the Center for Discovery in Harris, New
York. Her skin still looks amazing.

THE CLOONEY. There once was a time when George Timothy
Clooney (b. 1961) was married. It was after his days on *The
Facts of Life* but before *ER* made him a household name. For a
few years beginning in 1989 he was married to actress Talia
Balsam, and he has made it clear in the years since that he
never plans to marry again. He doesn't vilify his ex-wife; instead he criticizes the institution of marriage itself. It's keen to
be able to separate the person from the establishment. I think
of someone like Kelsey Grammer, who entered his fourth marriage in 2011. A year later, he did an interview with Oprah and
refused to even say his third ex-wife's name (*Real Housewives of
Beverly Hills* star Camille Donatacci). His bitterness was palpable. Marriage is funny that way—you don't necessarily get
better at it the more often you do it. You can say, "I married the
wrong person" until kingdom come. If you don't stop and self-

examine, other people will always be the wrong people. Clooney took an internal inventory and decided that marriage just
wasn't for him. George Clooney is committed to his films, his
charity work, and I believe he is completely committed to his
girlfriends—for about two years. (If anyone knows how to get
me on the shortlist to be his next girl, I'm all ears. 'Preciate it.)

A FEW MORE NEVER-MARRIEDS: Queen Elizabeth I, Galileo
Galilei, Sir Isaac Newton, Ludwig van Beethoven, Jane Aus-
ten, Henry David Thoreau, Susan B. Anthony, Florence
Nightingale, Louisa May Alcott, Vincent van Gogh, Mary
Cassatt, The Wright brothers (neither of 'em), Greta Garbo,
Jean-Paul Sartre, Simone de Beauvoir, Ralph Nader, Oprah
Winfrey, Daryl Hannah, Kylie Minogue

> *I don't think that because I'm not married it's made my life any*
> *less. That old maid myth is garbage.*
>
> —Diane Keaton

EIGHT

UNREQUITED
PLATONIC LOVE

*I have no duty to be anyone's Friend and no man in the world has
a duty to be mine. No claims, no shadow of necessity. Friendship
is unnecessary, like philosophy, like art, like the universe itself (for
God did not need to create). It has no survival value; rather it is
one of those things which give value to survival.*

—C. S. Lewis, *The Four Loves*

Friendships go through many of the same twists, turns,
and dismal periods that romantic relationships do. Platonic loyalty is just as powerful as amorous loyalty and Platonic
betrayal, just as wounding. In friendship, there's often the same
strong sense of not being able to live without someone while
simultaneously being aware that they can drive you absolutely
crazy. A friend knows, as a significant other knows, exactly
where your buttons are and how to push them; if they want
to flip an insecure switch, for instance, they have access to
it. Friends often have valuable insights into our psyche and

situations long before we do. They can also say things that leave us deflated for days. At times we have the intense desire to change our friends, while other moments we are in complete harmony and couldn't ask for a human who knows us better.

There can even be an infatuation period with friendship, marked by excitement minus the desire to jump on top of the person every time you see them. In his book *The Four Loves*, C. S. Lewis points out that we do not need friendship to reproduce and it was once considered the most important love for that reason—it is chosen freely, with no biological basis. I believe the excitement of a new friendship comes from spotting a mental mirror image. In this person you see characteristics that you possess or that you would very much like to possess. As with biologically based infatuation, however, new-friend infatuation can be dangerous. We are tempted to think: This new friend is rad, amazing, and sooooo much better than all my old friends. In the presence of newness it's easy to leave old friends behind—the ones who've been there for you for many years.

Due to the similarities between the two types of love, many of same rules apply to flailing friendships as do to troubled romance. As with romance, it's important to recognize that your friends are in your life because they choose to be. If you sense them backing away, it's not your job to hunt them down and beg them to stay. You have every right to confront them and ask what's going on, but if they've subconsciously decided that they're done with you, they might not give you the courtesy of a sit down. A while back I noticed a girlfriend avoiding me at every chance, but she was so friendly about it—always promising we'd see each other next time. I finally asked, "Are you still upset with me over that argument we had months ago?" She confessed she was and that she needed us to take a break. At first I was annoyed that she didn't just say that from the start, but I realized it was something she hadn't put her finger on yet. It was an interesting tribute to how well I knew her that I zeroed in on what was bothering her before she did. It felt right when we parted ways. Knowing the truth, even the difficult truth, is better than living in limbo.

The flip side of this is when you begin to sense that a friend is no longer good for you or, perhaps, never has been. Our insecurities can lead us to toxic friendships the same way they do toxic romance and keep us there for longer than is healthy. We can be drawn to a person's charisma only to learn that she is condescending and controlling. Because of the initial magnetism, however, we might think that it's our problem and continue to try and please that person. *She makes me feel bad, but I still want her approval.* There we go again—trying to mooch our sense of self off another person.

We tend to think of the end of relationships as failure, and the fear of failure won't allow us to give up. "But we've been friends for so long" we say to ourselves. As with so many other situations, we're afraid to lose the past or the future. A friendship that's lasted for years is something to be proud of. If the two of you have evolved into different people, though, and it's a struggle to remain part of each other's lives, then there's nothing wrong with going your separate ways. Sometimes friendships end and it's no one's fault. Other times, it's no one's fault but one party takes it personally and feels the need to blame. If a friend ridicules you as you walk away, consider it confirmed that you did the right thing.

One major difference between eros and friendship is how they are maintained. Erotic love needs to be tended to, like a wood-burning fire, whereas friendship can survive great distance and long periods of time apart. Those moments when you haven't seen a friend in ages and pick up as if you were together just yesterday are pure magic. Since friendship can survive time and distance, I encourage you to leave room for life changes in your friends' lives. You will lose them for a while when they have children. Even when you're with them conversation goes something like, "How are you? Charlie put that down! I'm sorry . . . how are you? Wait. Where is he? I'll be right back." Be patient and supportive, they will be back someday.

Friendship enters dramatic territory when there's new love in someone's life. It's especially interesting when a guy friend brings a new girl around. The moment of truth comes: Is she or isn't she okay with him having girl friends? They always say they don't mind at first. When it's you who has the new love, introducing him to your friends is ideally a joy. Unfortunately this situation is rife with potential minefields. If your friends don't think the guy is treating you right, there will be a struggle. Or maybe your friends are the bad guys and they make fun of him (per my Memorial Day story). Sometimes these conflicts are bad enough to end a friendship. It's true, certain friendships need to end, but be careful about ending a friendship under the influence of a new relationship or even a new friendship. Try, as best you can, to remember if you ever wanted out of this friendship before the new person came along. It's a gift to have inspiring people enter your life, but don't give them the benefit of every doubt just because they're new. They have to prove themselves, which your tried-and-true friends have already done.

Of course the double whammy, the knife in the back, *and* the heart condition, is when a friend is intimate with your current or former lover. This happened to me in high school. During my junior year, my boyfriend broke up with me unexpectedly. He was the first boy I adored while we were seeing each other—no admiring from a distance or dating him just because I thought I was supposed to. (And I'm sure this was a direct result of him being a troublemaker.) Two weeks after the breakup my girlfriend, Clara, called me and said, "So . . . Shawn stopped by to see me the other night." There was no yelling, just silence on the phone. In the days that followed she kept saying she wouldn't see him anymore and she kept seeing him.

In this situation you have two choices: end the friendship or forgive your friend and continue on. I went with option C, which was to not forgive her, remain her friend, and remind her as often as possible what a terrible person she was. I would've ended the friendship if I knew for certain our friends would choose sides; with a guarantee that she'd be abandoned, I would've enacted that punishment immediately. The more likely scenario, however, was that our friends would give us equal billing. Unable to banish her, I used guilt to persuade her to do things for me. (She had her driver's license a year before I did.) This wasn't the right thing to do—at all—but I officially no longer hold myself accountable for that which I did in high school. My attempts to make her feel bad lasted a few months; then I forgave and moved on naturally. By senior year, she was still seeing Shawn and the three of us even palled around together. One summer afternoon, they invited me into a three-some. It didn't happen. When the moment arrived she was un-comfortable,* but I was flattered just the same.

Unfortunately, I believe this double-trouble betrayal hap-pens more often than anyone wants to believe it does and well beyond high school. The August 2009 issue of *Psychology Today*, which focused on jealousy, reported, "Over fifty percent of males and females report having tried to steal a friend's part-ner." When you're married, you spend time with your married friends. Sometimes they're the only new people you see and it's possible for a line to be crossed. In the book *Perfection: A Mem-oir of Betrayal and Renewal*, author Julie Metz tells the story of her husband dying of a sudden heart attack one January day. In the months that followed she discovered that he had been hav-ing affairs with several women, her friend Cathy among them.

The ability to tell the loyal friends from the untrustworthy ones lies within; same goes for recovering if a once-loyal friend becomes a sudden betrayer. The better sense of self you have, the more likely you are to connect with and attract those who have similar interests and see the world the way you do. You'll also know beyond a reasonable doubt when the time has come to end a friendship. If you choose to go through this process, keep in mind another mistruth we learn from fairytales: there are only two roles people can play, villain or hero. Each of us has it in us to play both characters—sometimes on the same day. Know that the day will come when a friend—even the

---

* Rightly so—this was one of the many things he wanted that she was willing to do just to please him.

best one—will let you down, and you will let her down. How it's handled might mean the end or a further strengthening of your bond.

The truth is, everyone is going to hurt you. You just got to find the ones worth suffering for.

—Bob Marley

FEIGNING FRIENDSHIP TO KEEP IN TOUCH WITH HIM

I have a lot of guy friends; more than most women I know. I love my boy friends—homosexual and hetero, alike. They make my life rich with perspective. To the disbelief of many, I have friendships with heterosexual men rounding the decade mark and we've never dated. We have no plans to date. We are friends through and through. Plenty of their girlfriends, some of them now wives, are accepting of this and have male friendships of their own to foster. I've also salvaged full friendship or genial acquaintanceship with men I've dated. It is the age of male/female friendship, and that is something to celebrate.

My natural inclination to befriend men, however, can be a problem. It can be a problem for all women—even those who don't have a whole herd of guy friends. When things don't work out as you'd hoped with the cad around the corner, it's very easy to say, "We'll be friends," and believe it. Even though you were never friends to begin with and he's made it clear with his actions that he can go on without seeing you and be just fine—you declare friendship to save yourself from having to deal with the uncomfortable quiet. It's difficult to have an intriguing person become part of your life and then face the silence after he leaves. *Yesterday we were having gripping conversations; now who am I supposed to talk to?* But it's best to talk to your existing friends—even though conversation won't be as mesmerizing. If you continue to seek out Danny Zuko under the guise of friendship, you're most likely going to end up back in bed together. Afterward, he will be completely satisfied while you want more—and more and more—as you continue to see him. If you catch yourself picking out his birthday present every time you're in Bergdorf's, no contact is best.

It's true that some magnificent, meaningful friendships are born of relationships that don't work out, but that should happen organically. If the desire to befriend him is genuine, it will still be there when your binoculars are pointed toward a new heartthrob. Perhaps get in touch with him then. Or maybe the need to befriend him will evaporate and you'll run into him shortly after it does. You have an unexpectedly cheery coffee chat and voilà, friends. Whatever you do, wait. Wait a month or two. Do not cling to the notion of friendship in the immediate aftermath of emotional defeat.

I've also done the opposite, where I assume friendship with men I've dated who I don't feel any passion for. The gentleman I dated shortly after seeing Indiana Jones on Halloween but before finding out he was engaged, for example. While we were dating, I thought we were laying the foundation for a friendship. I kept thinking, When this doesn't work out, we'll be friends. (It's not a frame of mind I'm willing to date with these days.) Things predictably ended and I pursued friendship. I waited a few weeks because we were both traveling, but then I invited him to get together. He responded positively and said he'd let me know when he's free. I then invited him to my birthday party. He never wrote to tell me he couldn't come; instead a mutual friend walked into the party and said he wouldn't be able to make it.

I was incensed. I wrote an e-mail, allowing myself to do it because I was certain my intentions were not romantic. The gist of the e-mail: "We had a super-honest relationship, why are you avoiding me? I don't care if you're dating anyone. Good for you if you are. I want to find out how your trip was and tell you about mine." I didn't send it to him, though. Instead I sent it to my friend Lori and asked her to show it to her husband, John. She wrote back, "John says . . . sometimes guys just want to go cold turkey. He says not to send the e-mail." So I didn't, and I'm glad I didn't. My ego didn't like being blown off even in a platonic way—that's all. The lesson is: There is no need to chase anyone down and talk them into being a part of your life— especially not a friend. A friend will be there without prodding.

A FRIEND IS JUST NOT THAT INTO YOU . . .

People begin friendships the way they begin relationships, on their best behavior. It takes time—more time with a friend since you don't see them as often as a lover—to let your guard down and be your true self. This is why we can wake up years into a friendship and wonder, How did I get here? I don't need to be treated this way. I've only ended one friendship in my life directly, where I told the person I didn't want to be in touch anymore. It was strange, and he was very confused. It was a friendship I knew better than to enter into the first place, but my propensity to be nice and give people the benefit of the doubt gets me in trouble. Fortunately, he introduced me to some great people. One of those people I remain good friends with, so there was positive gain.

It took me a long time to identify what it was that bothered me, and I finally homed in on it; he was constantly telling me how to improve my life. An occasional suggestion from a friend about something I might do is welcome, but this was incessant. It was also very friendly and not outwardly critical, which is why it was difficult to spot in the first place. His advice went something like this: "You must speak with so-and-so about so-and-so." "Why do you choose to do that when you could be doing this instead?" "Oh you should work in sales. You would be fantastic in sales." If he'd bothered to get to know me he would've known I'd rather be drawn and quartered than work in sales. He once sent me an e-mail telling me exactly how much money I needed to be making at this point in my life. After that, I determined that I didn't think my life needed nearly as much improving as he thought it did. It was time to go.

He did not take the news well. I tried to explain that we just have different styles of friendship, but he was astonished. He genuinely believed he was being helpful. He continues to call me every six to eight months and leave a voicemail as if nothing had happened, "Oh we must get together and catch up." I would return his call if I thought we could have a reasonable conversation and I could explain again that I wish him all the best but don't care for us to be in touch anymore. Alas, the fact that he continues to call—with all calls unanswered—proves that there is no room for reason.

Most of the time, ending a friendship does not take this type of effort. Usually the fade-away will do. If you do find yourself having to flat out tell another person you no longer want to be friends, hopefully they won't continue to call you. Here are a few conventional ways to tell if the end is near:

YOU'RE DOING ALL THE WORK. It may occur to you that if you stop calling this person, it's likely you will never hear from her again. If that's the case, stop calling. Or if the relationship is one-sided in other ways—you find yourself doing all the favors and receiving nothing in return—there's no need to keep it up. All you have to do is say no to several favors in a row and this friend will find someone else to mooch off.

S/HE IS ENDLESSLY CRITICAL. If you find a friend puts you down more often than she lifts you up, be bold and walk away. This situation might require more than the fade-away because the emotional sadist needs the masochist. A person who likes to belittle will notice when her punching bag has gone missing. Without being critical—demonstrate how it's done—explain how often you find yourself hurt by this friendship and that it's in your best interest to end it. If she criticizes you, keep walking and don't turn back.

YOU ARE LEFT BEHIND EACH AND EVERY TIME S/HE FALLS IN LOVE. What's unfortunate about this situation is that any person who leaves loyal friends when there's a new man in town suffers from low self-esteem. A person who is strong on all sides recognizes that friendship contributes to the well-lived life just as much as new love and will work to maintain both. Once can be forgiven, but if your friend leaves you in the dust regularly because of dating, you will be doing her a favor by not being there when she comes back. This is one lesson she'll have to learn the hard way.

YOU'RE FRIENDS WITH EDDIE HASKELL. There can be "friends" who thrive on making you do things they know make you uncomfortable. Maybe this person doesn't care about your new demanding job and insists you stay out until three a.m. like you did when you were twenty-five. Any attempts you make to leave are met with name-calling and put-downs. If you tolerate disrespectful behavior it will get worse over time. Tell Eddie you were glad to have spent your younger years with him, but it's time to go our separate ways.

> *Keep away from people who try to belittle your ambitions. Small people always do that, but the really great make you feel that you, too, can become great.*
>
> —Mark Twain

MY BEST FRIEND'S DIVORCE

I once had a friend. He was my friend-turned-boyfriend-turned-basically-brother. We met in undergrad in the fall of 1998. We were friends for two years and then dated from 2000 to 2002. Toward the end of our relationship, I wasn't a good girlfriend. Working as a waitress, I gave in to temptation one night and stayed afterward to have my way with the sous chef in the private dining room. My boyfriend then became my ex-boyfriend, but we miraculously returned to friendship when the pain had passed. As it turned out, I'm a great ex-girlfriend. I am the Jimmy Carter of ex-girlfriends.

My old chum is a stand-up comedian and, for storytelling purposes, I christen him Ricky Ricardo. I knew our true fate was to be friends within a year of our breakup. His career started to gain momentum and he called me from the road regularly with female conquest stories. They didn't ignite a flare of possessiveness within me; rather, I listened attentively and provided feedback as needed. Over the years our friendship deepened in a way our romantic relationship couldn't because we ran to each other with our hearts broken in our hands. We liked to introduce each other as, "My ex-girlfriend/ex-boyfriend" just for reaction's sake. During those days he went from being a waiter to a full-time comedian, and I had my first articles and books published. We had a momentous decade together.

The end began in early 2008 after he ran into a girl we went to college with. "Do you remember Lucy the Zeta?" he asked on the phone.

"Yes."

"We've been having lots of sex this week."

Other than his blasé description, I thought nothing of it—it sounded like business as usual. Lucy started petitioning for a serious relationship shortly after their week of lust. Ricky said he was reluctant but his actions suggested otherwise as he steered his car in her direction often. By March, things were on the verge of official. When Ricky enters a romantic relationship it requires two conversations. The first is the standard, "Let's be exclusive." The second goes something like, "I'm good friends with my ex-girlfriend." With Lucy, as with the others chosen for exclusivity, the second conversation came immediately after the first. As relayed to me, she took a deep breath and said she understood.

Within months, Lucy moved to Queens, a few blocks away from Ricky. I applauded their decision not to move in together immediately. Over the phone I heard all about the move, Lucy's job hunt, and the cross-country drive they took together. Ricky boasted about the trip with, "She didn't get on my nerves at all!" Dopamine does it again. Everything appeared to be going well, and for the first five months of their relationship I had no idea there was a problem—let alone that *I* was the problem.

The truth revealed itself one July night. I'd invited them both to a reading I was doing on the Lower East Side and only Ricky showed up. We met outside before the reading and agreed to head to a diner afterward. I told him the reading would be over around ten. "Sounds good," he replied. "I have to be home at eleven." I thought I misunderstood, so I repeated myself, "The reading will be over at ten." He repeated himself. I raised my eyebrows and asked why we could only hang out for forty-five minutes. His face gave way—a little boy with his hand in the cookie jar. "She's uncomfortable with this," he confessed. I glared at him. I was mostly annoyed that this was the first time I was hearing Lucy had a problem with our friendship. I told him there was no need to wait for me; if he had a curfew then he had a curfew. He called the next day to assure me everything would be okay.

Soon we were back to our regular phone chats. I was kept abreast of his auditioning for a movie role and Lucy attending an event at the Playboy Club, hoping to be selected for the magazine. Ever the good boyfriend, Ricky bragged as if it were an imminent possibility. The next time I saw him in person, it was late fall. He was performing at The Comedy Cellar, and we met before the show for coffee. Lucy called shortly after we sat down. I didn't think there was anything unusual with the first call, but when the second, third, and forth calls came in, I knew something was up. Between her calls and frantic texts he would assure me (or himself), "She's not crazy. She's really not crazy. It's only ex-girlfriends she gets upset about." I smiled sympathetically. The thing about insecurity is, it doesn't fit neatly into a box; it's more of a blue-ink-type substance that leaks and splatters everywhere at inconvenient times. That night he said to me, "If I have to choose between you and her, I'll choose you. And, no offense, but I'm not choosing *you*, I'm choosing the principle. She can't tell me who I can be friends with." Wise words.

After that episode, I knew not to wait for him to volunteer information, so I started asking for it. As time went on, my inquiries were met with reluctance or lies. By mid-2009 our friendship was eroding. A few of the things he said to me during this period: "There are things I don't tell you because I want you to like her." "What you have to understand about Lucy is she's an only child. She's under the influence of her friends." And my personal favorite: "This would be easier if you had a boyfriend!" "You mean this is my fault?" I said to myself. "Awesome." If he'd said that just a few years earlier it would have crushed me, but I was starting to catch on; that statement said more about his relationship status than it said about mine. I pointed out what a shitty thing it was to say. He apologized.

Apparently the story he had been telling Lucy—and buying into himself—is that I was just like one of his guy friends. I was like one of the guys in that he and I don't have sex and I like *X-Men*, *Star Trek*, *Star Wars*, and *Lord of the Rings*. By my chromosome determination, however, I'm a woman and there are bound to be things that bother me that don't bother boys. Whenever I tried to tell him how hurtful his lies were, his response was, "Why can't you be more like Keith?" I suggested he change his analogy to brother and sister.

Speaking of *X-Men*, there is a great exchange that takes place in the first movie. Wolverine says to Cyclops, "You gonna tell me to stay away from your girl?" and Cyclops comes back with, "If I had to do that, she wouldn't be my girl." Exactly! All hail comic book wisdom. If you feel it's your responsibility to shield your significant other's eyes from passersby and tell him what to do rather than trust his ability to make the right decisions, you've already lost. I couldn't believe Ricky didn't see what an enormous lack of trust she was exhibiting with her attempts to control him. Maybe he did and didn't want to have yet another argument.

Against all odds, the three of us managed to sit down for brunch one morning. I didn't sense any hostility—honestly, none. The conversation was lively and each of us participated equally. Ricky paid for the three of us, which I thought was a nice nod to how much he'd wanted this event to take place. Hope was on the horizon. He asked for her hand in marriage in late 2009. I sent a congratulations card. Ricky told me the wedding would be in October 2010 and to "save the date."

The summer before the wedding, my cousin Kate and I were traveling. "I'm not so sure I'm going to be invited to this wedding," I told her. Kate assured me that I would. Everyone who had known Ricky and me for all ten years of our friendship assured me that I would. People who had never met him, however, and heard me tell the story were much more doubtful. Then, suddenly, I was invited. A month before the wedding I got a text message at two a.m. that read, "Send me your address ASAP for a wedding invite." I did as I was asked. Instead of receiving an invitation, however, I received an e-mail one week later in which Ricky told me that after much thought, I wouldn't be invited after all.

Not being invited is one thing, but dealing the fatal blow to our twelve-year friendship over e-mail was atrocious. Also, I'd been semi-prepared not to be invited to the wedding—until he invited me. The disinvite was unexpected and cruel. I was devastated for three days. Then I was relieved. I realized that I didn't have to listen to him lie to me anymore or hear about her accusing me of having feelings that I didn't have. The friendship I was holding on to no longer existed. I also realized that I'd had it in me to walk away much sooner. Moving forward, if someone asks me if I can be more like someone else, I'm going to say no and take my leave. Don't get me wrong, Keith is a great guy—salt of the earth—but the only person I have it in me to be is me. The moment my friends start asking for someone else is the moment they stop being a friend.

In the midst of all this, my friend Rich wrote me the greatest e-mail. Ever.

Samara,

Let me get right into it: this is ridiculous—and he's going to regret it. He is, of course, operating under the assumption that, since he'll have the splendid (I'm sure) Lucy for the rest of his life, he won't really need his friends. Many have made this mistake and found themselves virtually friendless when their marriages or relationships imploded. Give it ten years: He'll be back, begging for forgiveness. They all do.

I'm reminded of an episode from Edith Wharton's *Age of Innocence*. While traveling in France, Newland Archer and his new bride, May, attend a dinner party where they meet a young man who works as a tutor. Newland and the tutor have "an awfully good talk after dinner about books and things," and Newland tells May he'd like to have the guy over to their place for dinner. May scoffs and, to Newland's chagrin, casts the deciding vote on the matter—a resounding no: "The little Frenchman? Wasn't he dreadfully common?" And then the third-person narrator breaks in with this passage, which I'll never forget: "[Newland] perceived with a flash of chilling insight that in the future many problems would be thus negatively solved for him." I think that Ricky's going to find the same thing: this is the first of many decisions that will be made for him. He couldn't find the courage to stand up for a friend of ten years . . . wow, just imagine what's in store for him! Stick a fork in the man—he's done. In other words, she's got him by the balls already!

Just look at it this way: no expensive gift; no subpar dinner; no stupid conversation with the inevitably inane tablemates; and, most important, no goddamned chicken dance and hokey poky. (I hate weddings.)

In fairness to Ricky, I believe he did stand up for our friendship. I think they fought about it often. After a while, however, the time comes to stop arguing and say to yourself: "I'm being asking to give up a friend. Am I going to do it?" and make your decision from a place of truth rather than continuing to deny that that's what is being asked of you. He never really made the decision. In his last e-mail to me he said, "I'd like to still communicate as friends." Hmmm, it's not exactly, "I still want us to be friends." I, on the other hand, was done. I waited a week to respond—so it wouldn't be an angry, reactionary response—and wished them both well.

Was I being unreasonable in thinking he and I could actually remain friends? I didn't expect things to stay the same—we were going to have to stop introducing each other as exes—but, yes, I did believe we could continue to be part of each other's lives. It's been done, after all. In a November 2011 article for *The Atlantic* entitled "All the Single Ladies," Kate Bolick wrote of an ex-boyfriend, "After the worst of our breakup, we eventually found our way to a friendship so deep and sustaining that several years ago, when he got engaged, his fiancée suggested that I help him buy his wedding suit. As he and I toured through Manhattan's men's-wear ateliers, we enjoyed explaining to the confused tailors and salesclerks that no, no, *we* weren't getting married."

I waited until the wedding photos were posted on Facebook so I could make fun of them (Lucy and I have drastically different taste) before ultimately unfriending him and unfollowing him on Twitter. This wasn't an act of malice but one of sadness. I didn't want to read the status updates of a friend whose home I was no longer welcome in. To satisfy my curiosity, however, I did Google him every five months or so. There was no harm in seeking updates on his career because he'll always have my support with that—even from a distance. I was there from the very beginning.

It was during one such routine act of Google that I happened upon some news—news that I expected to hear someday, but not this day. I began to type his name into everyone's favorite search engine and it auto-populated the word divorce. *Hmm, that's curious.* "Ricky Ricardo Divorce." I hit search and ended up on his Wikipedia page. This line had been added to the bio: "Ricardo was married in 2010 to Lucille Esmeralda McGillicuddy; the pair divorced in 2012." I had little to no hope for this relationship, but I figured she'd boss him around for many years before he'd finally had enough.

I thought of my old friend Jack. That man had more second thoughts than a first-time bungee jumper. He practically proclaimed divorce a month before his big day. He is still married. While there were red flags abound with Ricky's relationship, he himself was steady as could be. He told me he couldn't have me at the wedding because, "I love her with all my heart." It's what any woman would want her fiancé to say. Perhaps his divorce occurred quickly because he, in fact, wasn't the one who wanted it. Men have been known to sit in the backseat on this decision; as it happens, women initiate two-thirds of all divorces in the United States, as was the case here.

In true twenty-first-century fashion, I got the answers to my questions from a podcast interview Ricky had given. In the course of the conversation he revealed that Lucy had called for the divorce. Apparently she told him that she hadn't wanted to get married in the first place (a-hem, then why all this worry over the guest list?) and that she was unhappy with the money he wasn't making (which means she married a stand-up comedian expecting career consistency). Ricky went to couples counseling alone for three months; she refused to go.

He concluded, and I acquiesced in front of my laptop, that she wanted a wedding and put no thought whatsoever into maintaining an actual marriage. Initially I'm sure both of them believed her jealousy was an expression of love. He was probably flattered, thinking, "Oh you'll have to excuse her. She loves me too much." In truth, it was evidence of her lack of love for herself—her attempts at any other type of love were fatally flawed.

As word of his divorce made its way around, a mutual friend e-mailed and asked, "Did you chuckle to yourself (mmmm-waaahhhh) when you heard the news? C'mon, it's me." I'll come clean: Of course I did! I'm working on abolishing my ego; the process is not yet complete. I wasn't happy about anyone's broken heart; it was more of a, "Dude you're my friend. I know when someone is bringing out the douche in you." During their dating days when Lucy was having a typical hissy fit about our spending time together, I wanted to scream, "Break up with him! Go ahead. I dare you. Guess what—I STILL won't date him. I haven't wanted to date him for six years. I wasn't waiting for you to come along to change my mind!" Oh how badly I wanted to write her and emphasize this, while complimenting her wedding-day beehive (the highest one I've ever seen), of course. Cooler cognition prevailed.

It's been about a year since I made the discovery. For now, I am firm in not getting in touch with Ricky.* It's his move to make. He ended our friendship therefore it's he who would have to attempt to reinstate it. I think it's dangerous, however, for me to assume that's what he wants. Maybe he decided we

---

* I reserve the right to change my mind.

outgrew each other, or that I'm too much of a liability for future relationships. It was wrong of Ricky and Lucy to assume, "Once *she's* gone our relationship will be problem free." Problems don't exist outside of people nearly as much as they exist inside of people. With that in mind, it would be unwise of me to think now that Lucy is out of the picture that things can go back to the way they were. Ricky and I would have to start over. Our reunion aside, I hope his sorrow has passed and that he knows by now that she did him a gargantuan favor. I've no doubt it made for some good material for him—as it has for me.

> *If someone is not treating you with love and respect, it is a gift if they walk away from you. If that person doesn't walk away, you will surely endure many years of suffering with him or her. Walking away may hurt for a while, but your heart will eventually heal. Then you can choose what you really want. You will find that you don't need to trust others as much as you need to trust yourself to make the right choices.*
>
> —Don Miguel Ruiz, *The Four Agreements*

LESS THAN FRIENDS

The expression "Let's be more than friends" implies that a long-term relationship or marriage is the next step up from friendship; it's an improvement on an already strong bond. But is a romantic relationship always an improvement over a friendship? In some areas, yes—no doubt that physical intimacy is a wondrous thing. In other areas, though, we may be closer to our friends.

Let's look at conversational intimacy. As a friend you are often asked to keep secrets for your friends in relationships—something a significant other doesn't know or, as you are told, can't know. It might be a series of minor irritations or a clandestine confession that has the potential to end it all if discovered. Many times, it's friends, rather than intimate partners we can say anything to and not fear judgment or an imminent argument. We celebrate marriage as the union of best friends, two people who can tell each other anything. I've seen the exception as often as I've seen the rule—where one or both parties lie to maintain order.

For this reason, I make a motion to reinstate friendship as a relationship equally as important as romance. The reigning philosophy now seems to be, "Friends are great but they pale in comparison to a husband or wife." But we can coexist without making one better than the other. With good friends around, your relationship may stand a better chance of survival or you may stand a better chance of survival if things end unexpectedly. In *The Four Loves*, C. S. Lewis asserts, ". . . to the Ancients, Friendship seemed the happiest and most fully human of all loves; the crown of life and the school of virtue. The modern world, in comparison, ignores it."

If friends are considered as important as spouses, they might not get left behind as often when married life begins. Again, it's necessary to end toxic friendships, but ending a friendship you had no desire to end before a new boyfriend came along is not just giving up the friend, it's giving up a part of yourself. Ricky, for example, had to leave his own integrity behind in order to get married and that sacrifice went completely unnoticed or appreciated by his new bride—which tells me it wasn't worth leaving behind in the first place.

Part of the reason I knew the relationship was troubled was because of all the lies required to maintain it. They weren't malicious lies meant to hurt but rather meant to protect. He was trying to protect me from getting my feelings hurt (didn't work) and protect himself from having limitless arguments with Lucy. The thing about lies is, the intention doesn't matter. Lies are lies. Love, platonic or erotic, is not the absence of conflict but rather the productive management of it. If you're lying just to avoid arguments then you are not assessing how you handle conflict together. Can you can both fight fair or agree to disagree when necessary? Can you tell the truth even when it's a difficult truth? Sometimes lies are meant to avoid figuring this out altogether, because if you realize for certain you can't handle conflict, there's not a lot of choice left but to end the relationship.

The more a person lies, the more likely they're dishonest with themselves. If you're not honest with yourself, it's impossible to be honest with anyone else—friend or object of affection. If you *are* honest with yourself, you're much more likely to tell the truth to your significant other as often as you do to your friends, and vice versa—making for more solid unions all around.

NINE

EXTINGUISHING
THE TORCH

There will come a time when you think everything is finished.
That will be the beginning.

—Louis L'Amour

You may have noticed that I repeat myself. There's a reason for it. We've had the same ideas drilled into our heads our whole lives: the whens; the hows; the what life should look like; the what love should look like. That love should be effortless and easy. It's difficult to let go of this because it's all we've ever heard. We've subscribed to the notions, "Of course it matters what they think," "My life will begin as soon as the right guy walks in the door," "Without a date, I am nobody," and "Every girl gets a big day." Therefore I repeat "Don't take it personally," "Love begins with you," "You are enough," and "Today is your day," to counter decades of hearing the exact opposite. I've been listening to the sweet sounds of these counter messages for three years, but I'm still combating the first thirty of thinking otherwise. Recognizing truth in these words is the first step—saying to yourself, "This way of thinking is going to serve me well." Know, however, that absorption is not automatic; it's the beginning of inner transformation. You have to continually remind yourself of these new methods because the old way of thinking will creep back in. Honestly, it's much easier to think the other way, but when the new system of thought starts to become instinctive, it's a glorious thing.

One old-school feeling associated with unrequited love is helplessness. We assume we are powerless against it and that's why we suffer. You have so much more control than you think you do, though. It's true that when we're addicted to loving someone, some thinking patterns are involuntary—as discussed in Chapter Four. You may be trying to control your thoughts and finding that you can't. No matter what's going on in your brain, however, you *can* control whether or not you seek help. Whether it's therapy, a support group, or self-help resources (books, periodicals, websites, etc.), exploring your issue can help you solve it.

In the meantime, let's make it our new method to try to stop the feelings of helplessness before they start. As soon as he stops calling, consider yourself done. Don't say, "What did I do wrong?" but rather, "That's inconsiderate of him and disrespectful to me. Done." If the man asks you out after class on Saturday and acts like you have food on your face the following Wednesday, you're done. That is going to be his problem, not yours. If he says, "I want this and I want this with you BUT . . ." you're done. There is no BUT when two people decide to give each other an authentic chance.

When I say, "You're done," I'm not saying, "Get over it!" I know there's no Off switch. I'm saying, acknowledge that it isn't happening instead of hoping that things will change. Skip the overanalyzing, intoxicated texting, cyber-stalking, and figuring out ways to run into him. Sit down and say to yourself, "He's not interested and that doesn't make me any less." Then be unhappy. Disappointed. Dejected. Feel the hurt. Process it as long as you need to. If it takes weeks, those are weeks spent getting over him rather than continuing to chase him and then having to get over him—the latter takes twice as long. If you chase, there's also a greater risk of embarrassing yourself by taking one of your attempts to win him too far (not that I would know anything about this). What if he comes back on bended knee? Deal with that if and when it happens and not a second before. Right now, you're done.

By walking away, it feels like giving up on love. It isn't, though; it's staying true to yourself. Staying with you—rather than handing it all over to him—will get you over it more quickly. It feels unnatural to do it this way, I know, and that's because of your ego. It's your ego's job to want what it can't have. All the ego cares about is the chase and proving other people wrong. Once it acquires what it wants, however, it will seek out something or someone else it can't have. It's time to cage that bastard and tell it, "Not this time." Love is the melding of what you want and what another person wants. If he doesn't even want to get things started, how could love be in the near future? I'm sorry if it hurts to hear that. If you follow it up with, "None of this makes me a bad person," it's easier to bear.

Let's make a deal. Try it my way, twice. I say twice because the first time isn't going to be smooth—there will be Facebook peeking or an illicit text. If you slip up the second time, try it once more. Aim to walk away from a man of intrigue as soon as he indicates he's not willing to move forward. Don't turn around—even digitally. If that doesn't ultimately make you feel like you just reached the emotional peak of Mt. Everest, you can go back to doing it the other way.

PRACTICING THE PREACH

I will now put my money where my mouth is; it's only fair. One summer afternoon I spotted a striking man from across the tent at a barbeque. I was standing next to the hostess when he said good-bye to her, and as soon as he walked away I eagerly inquired, "Who is he?" She told me he was her husband's friend and colleague at an architecture firm. Reading my intentions, she also said, "I'll set it up for you." It was a considerate offer, but I thought it unlikely that he'd want to get together with the girl he didn't meet at the barbeque.

To my pleasant surprise, I was wrong. Two weeks later Frank wrote me with a charming and forthright invitation to happy hour. We met on a rainy Thursday. He walked right up to me and gave me a friendly hug. I asked him how he knew what I looked like and he replied, "Julie sent me your Google image page." Oh right—that. How did half–blind dates happen before the Internet? Our conversation took off like a 1972 Maserati Merak. I stayed two hours longer than originally planned and my attempts to head home were met with, "Will you stay?" "Will you please stay?" "Will you have one more drink with me?" The evening ended with another scrumptious hug and him playing coy: "Yeah I guess I'll see you again." I liked him at once.

It is a well-known dating practicality that the interest scale is often tipped more heavily toward one person. It's worth being honest with yourself about this sooner rather than later. If the boy is more interested in you than you are in him, be careful with his feelings. If you sense that you're the more interested one, be careful with yours. While gauging my excitement level (extremely high), I decided that I would not put Frank's name in my phone. If we decided to be together (i.e., exclusive) then I would, but not before. This obviously won't work if you're dating several people at once—it's too many numbers to keep track of—alas, I was just seeing him. Seeing his number pop up made me just as gooey as seeing his name would have, but it was a reminder that we were still just getting to know each other.

Suspecting myself to be the more interested of we two, I implemented another rule: I wouldn't initiate contact—I would wait to hear from him. A friend asked me, "Why are you making him do all the work?" I wasn't. After our first date, he sent me an e-mail saying he had a great time and "I hope to see you again soon." I wrote back and said I was going to a restaurant opening next week and invited him to come. He accepted warmly.

Let's review: I waited to hear from him, and when I did, I was enthusiastic and upfront. He didn't mind that he had to be the one to reach out. At the end of all our dates he said, "I'll be in touch." I found this adorable—he wasn't committing to call-

ing, texting, or e-mail—just being in touch in one of those ca-
pacities. We also didn't become Facebook friends, which
thrilled me. I wanted to get to know him organically and not
come to conclusions based on a virtual scrapbook. I completely
approve of using Facebook to prod a man—let him know you
like him. Since there was no need for that here, I was glad to
leave it out.

The first time I spent the night at his place, it had been
some time since I had—how shall we say—carnal knowledge
of a man. I had no intention of telling him how long it had
been (and I'm not putting it in writing, either), but it came up
during the safe sex conversation. In that capacity, I felt assured
telling him. I was self-conscious about it otherwise until he
wrote the next day to tell me he was still sore and "I'm honored
you picked me." I was beyond excited that that's how he chose
to look at it; the other option being, "What's her problem?" It
was true. I was being selective and trying to take better care of
myself. The first time he spent the night at my place he brought
and left a brand-new toothbrush. I hoped it was because he
planned to stick around for a while. One date later, he was
gone.

All of our dates went well except the last one. Technically
speaking, nothing went wrong, but there was a noticeable distance. I used to panic when I sensed distance and would try to
shoo it out the door. The problem with this is distance is intan-
gible—it won't be shooed. Instead, it's best to acknowledge to
yourself that Casper the Distant Ghost is in the room and wait
and see what happens. We said good-bye on a Sunday afternoon. I didn't realize it right away, but in retrospect I noticed
that he didn't say his thing. He didn't say, "I'll be in touch."

That was the extent of the overanalyzing I did. I told myself I'd wait until Thursday before affirming it was over. Waiting a week makes sense, too, but our communication had been consistent enough that not hearing from him in four days would be telling.

Thursday came with no word from him and I accepted that that was that. It had been two months since our first date. I turned an irritated eye toward the universe, and she was ready for me. With her hands on her hips she said, "You didn't think I was going to give you this skill set without making sure you could use it, did you?" In these cases it isn't a matter of "You know what to do," as much as "You know what not to do." Here we go:

- Do not blame yourself.
- Do not ask "What's wrong with me?"
- Do not check his Facebook page.
- Do not call, text, e-mail, or write him any letters.
- Do not dwell on the words, "I'm honored you chose me." (It's true he said that and it was a nice thing to say, but the moment had passed and in order for a relationship to continue, such sentiments need to be reinforced with words and actions.)
- Do not plan to wait three months and get in touch with him again.
- Do not bring him up when you see your mutual friends.
- Do not ask him if he wants to be friends.

And I didn't. I didn't do any of it. What I did do was come up my own impromptu way of processing. He'd left four especially cute voice messages that I saved, so I listened to one message per day for the next four days and deleted each one afterward. I threw away his toothbrush. His number made its way out of my phone. I printed our e-mails, put them in my box of letters, and then deleted them. I keep certain e-mails for posterity's sake and for writing's sake. If you don't do that, you can just delete them—provided deleting is something that helps you move on. There was nothing to do Facebook wise. I hadn't written about him in my journal, so I decided I would delineate each date. At first I was very detailed in my descriptions and emoting all over the page. Toward the end it felt like a chore, which I thought was good.

A coworker asked how things were going and I gave her the update. She said, "You had feelings after only two months?" Determined not to be defensive I simply said, "Yes, I had feelings." I'm going to get defensive here. People decide to get married in two months and sometimes it works out. I would argue the opposite—if you don't have feelings after two months, maybe consider if you really like this person. Although, a friend of a friend did once tell me she doesn't know how she feels until around six months. We all have different dating compasses. The key is to know yourself. I know that if I'm going to feel something, it will be early on.

Lori's husband John questioned why I didn't give it one more try. "You could have called him," he said. "Every woman has one last phone call before she's considered crazy." I agree, and I followed that philosophy for a while. I would send one final text or e-mail just so the guy couldn't say, "Well, you could have contacted me." If you want to take that approach, I support it, but be firm with yourself beforehand and say,

"This is my final attempt." It's true, I could've called Frank, and we may even have gotten together once more. I had that very scenario play out a few times. After the get-together you initiate, however, you then have to deal with not hearing from him, so I just decided not to prolong the inevitable. When Frank wanted to see me, he got in touch. When he didn't, he didn't.

This probably isn't the ending you wanted. It wasn't the ending I wanted either. The point, nonetheless, isn't for me to always get what I want but rather to make the most of what comes my way. I didn't move on at warp speed. It took a few weeks before I stopped hoping it was the number-with-no-name every time my phone rang. The miracle took place when I did get over it. I was done in a way I've never been done before. I have memories of Frank and I can access them if I want to, but there is no emotional attachment to those recollections. There was no seeing his face in my cereal bowl for an indefinite amount of time afterward. I was astounded. I still have rope burns on my hands from holding on to some of the other men so tightly.

I must note that these were the post-Lexapro days, so it may have been all that super-succulent serotonin in my brain making this possible. I can say this: Falling for him didn't feel any different than it has when I've *really* fallen before, and being upset not to hear from him didn't feel any different initially either. The two differences were A) Surplus serotonin and B) I accepted it was over as soon as it was over. It felt like total team-work between modern medicine and me. The results were astonishing; there was no open-ended obsession. I did it. I liked him—a whole freakin' lot—but I never lost myself in the process.

Months later I received an unprompted update on Frank. Sometime in the fall a friend texted, "We ran into Frank at the Eagles game. He was incoherently drunk and dressed like a tool. Maybe it was for the best." It was for the best. Not just because he was wasted or dressed toolishly, though those details are always amusing, but because he wasn't interested. That's all. Now that I'm removed from it I'll say I'm glad I met Frank. We had a nice time together. The carnal knowledge was brilliant. It was meant to be a midsummer something, and that's what it was. I wouldn't be surprised to find out he's engaged or married. As a matter of fact, I've decided that moving forward, if I stop hearing from a man, I'm going to assume it's *because* he's getting married. He's not calling because he's too busy (with the seating chart). He's going through a really tough time right now (with his soon-to-be mother-in-law). He's afraid of commitment (to lavender tablecloths). He's a little too flirtatious (with the bridesmaids). Congratulations, Frank. I see your cab light is working.

> *. . . you know me, if there's one thing I like more than a refreshing beverage, it's serotonin.*
>
> —Dr. Sheldon Cooper, from CBS's *The Big Bang Theory*

THE POWER OF PERSPECTIVE

One night, back at the Campbell Apartment, a fellow hostess told me about her father. She said when she and her sister would bicker he often pulled a coin out of his pocket and held it between them. He presented the question, "What do you see?" Each little girl would describe to the best of her ability the side of the coin she saw. He would then ask, "Who's right?" and ultimately turn the coin over to assure them they both were.

This early lesson in perspective that my friend remembered fondly is a moral that our egos cannot comprehend. The ego will not allow other people to have their own perspectives. It must be right! That's one way to tell when your ego is behind the wheel—it's upset at others simply for seeing a situation differently. If you kick your ego to the curb you are free to believe what you believe while allowing others to do the same. You can even have a spirited debate while holding each other in high regard. When you feel the need to be right, rise within you, breathe, and remind yourself that the other person has, and is allowed to have, a different perspective—it's not going to bite. If you get too worked up and can't back down, change the subject.

We all have it in us to look at things differently—it's a matter of wanting to. We tend to get stuck on our side of the coin and if we stay too long, fear develops. It's the fear of even looking at the other side because, "What if I change my mind?" Oh ye of little faith. Trust yourself. Sometimes reading an article you disagree with further affirms what you do believe or gives you an appreciation for another point of view—even though your opinion remains the same. If you change your mind, you were meant to. Sometimes I change my mind and am not only glad I did but frightened that there's a chance I might have remained trapped in the old perspective. Don't be afraid to explore. Don't believe something just because it's the only option you've exposed yourself to. Look at a situation from several sides and choose the side that suits you. Then allow others to have their perspectives. It's exhausting to insist that everyone see things your way.

A willingness to turn the coin over can improve not only dinner conversations but also undesirable circumstances. I was given a chance to flex my perspective muscles one time when I was on an early-evening flight, headed home. The flight attendant announced that we would be landing late, which meant that I would miss my connecting flight. I immediately became frustrated and my thought process went like this: But. How. This is. Shit. Okay. Stop. Breathe. Can I control the situation? Boeing 757. Nope. Can't control it. Worst case: I miss my connecting flight, find a Starbucks in the airport, and write. I actually need to write. I could use a chai tea latte also. If I go home, I'm just going to go to sleep. This could work out. I could miss my flight. In five minutes I went from being annoyed to wanting the delay. Naturally, once my mind changed we landed on time, and that worked, too. If you can change a situation, do so. If not, work with what you've got. Complaining is wasted energy.

An adjustment in perspective can also help us take control of the disparaging thoughts we think. "What's wrong with me?" transforms into, "There is no one else like me!" Hurt becomes a lesson learned. Rejection is the universe saying, "You can do better." Failure becomes opportunity. The loss of love becomes the chance to love more deeply. "I will never," becomes "I'm not interested at the moment, but I try not to limit myself." Feeling assaulted by the Valentine's Day display at

CVS becomes a chance to buy a card for a family member or friend who you know could use a pick-me-up. The caterpillar becomes a butterfly. The mind opens and the shackles of "should, must, guilt, and shame" fall off. The power to do this is all up in your head.

In my early twenties, I was very proud of the fact that I had no plans to go back to school. I felt that I had found my calling and pitied the pour souls who hadn't. Ah, the perspectives of youth. In early 2011, on a beach in Honduras, my cousin Kate asked me a perspective-altering question. A little background first: Kate has logged in at least three thousand hours of her life listening to me analyze people. I analyze the men I've dated, the women they date, friends, foes, families, celebrities, and politicians. I must have been analyzing someone, don't remember who, and she enthusiastically interrupted, "Would you ever study psychology?" What an interesting idea. I liked it. I enjoyed the thought of listening to people and being an emotional guide. But then I dismissed it; I was overwhelmed by the time and money it would take to get my degree. I concluded that it was a good idea but not for me. Fortunately, my then-conclusion didn't matter; the seed had been planted.

In the months that followed I thought about my therapist. She wasn't a psychologist but a licensed clinical social worker, which is a social worker trained in psychotherapy. I looked into it and discovered that being an LCSW requires a master's degree in social work and two licenses. This seemed like a good way to go. A year and a half after the question had been asked, I was buying books for an MSW program set to begin that fall.

Although I am on my way to an MSW, at press time I was not there yet: no master's degree and no license. I am NOT a mental health professional of any kind. I write this book based on my own experience and the reading I have done. I am, however, headed toward earning a degree and am very excited about it. This is the path that has chosen me. There are a few years of school and training ahead, but in due time I hope to offer a safe haven to the misguided, broken hearted, dejected, and anyone who just needs to talk. Once again the universe (as funneled through Kate—thanks, Kate) was right about my career path, and I had the distinct pleasure of being wrong.

Let life happen to you. Believe me: Life is in the right, Always.

—Rainer Maria Rilke

A SPOONFUL OF CYNICISM

Perspective can be changed on purpose or by accident. The latter happens when life decides we are going to look at a situation from a different angle whether we want to or not. This is what happened to my perspective on marriage. While it's never been my sole ambition, I was certainly dreamy-eyed and looking forward to it. Then came Jack. He expressed reservations about his upcoming nuptials so candidly—until he got caught. Then he cowered like a soaking-wet kitten in the corner—shivering and terrified of his own opinion. Then there was Ricky. It wasn't simply that he had to lose his best friend in order to get married; he had to succumb to being treated badly during the entire wedding-planning process. Everybody dismissed him, including his fiancée. Eventually, even *he* resigned himself to thinking, "I'm just the groom, who cares about me?" I understand the groom usually doesn't give a damn about how the napkins are folded, but for the entire focus to be on the celebration and to all but write off the person with whom you are about to be united is beyond backward.

From the perch of my new perspective, it seemed marriage required people to check their individuality at the threshold, and I didn't like it. Of course, relationships require compromise and adjustments. I'm onboard with that, but to have to hide all evidence of who you once were in order to please your soon-to-be-spouse seems regrettably counterintuitive. To support my new point of view, I started seeking out the seedy side of marriage—evidence of unhappily ever after. It's easy to find and satisfyingly devious—like cheating on the status quo. I enjoyed movies such as *Revolutionary Road* and *Blue Valentine* (both very well written and acted if you can handle an unhappy ending). In late 2010, Arianna Huffington teamed up with writer/director Nora Ephron to launch *The Huffington Post* Divorce section, where I would go to for a daily dose of schadenfreude. I even started contributing to the *HuffPo* Divorce section. After a few contributions, my friend Scott said, "I'm starting to notice a theme . . ." These are the titles of four blog posts I wrote in succession for *HuffPo* Divorce: "The Myth of the Attractive Mistress" / "How Many Marriages Actually End in Happily Ever After?" / "Interview with an Adulterer" / "My Ex Invited Me into His Open Marriage."

Shortly after he brought it up, I decided it might be a good time to dial it back a little. I reminded myself that there are healthy marriages aplenty in my life—friends, family, and, of course, my parents. While I wasn't going to allow my pendulum to swing all the way back to delusional, having it hover over neutral felt right. As the weight of my perspective started to swing back, however, I changed my mind. I chose to pocket some of my pessimism. I looked to the late-eighteenth-century political philosopher William Godwin for guidance—because that's how I roll—and I decided there is no harm in harboring some cynicism.

I first encountered Godwin (1756–1836) my senior year of college in British Literature class. I have forgotten many of the other names and readings from that year, but Godwin's story stood out to me. In 1793 he wrote his first major work entitled *Enquiry Concerning Political Justice and Its Influence on Morals and Happiness*, and he included a bit on marriage. Here's what he had to say:

> The evil of marriage, as it is practiced in European coun-
> tries, extends further than we have yet described. The
> method is, for a thoughtless and romantic youth of each sex,
> to come together, to see each other, for a few times, and
> under circumstances full of delusion, and then to vow to
> eternal attachment. What is the consequence of this? In al-
> most every instance they find themselves deceived. They are
> reduced to make the best of an irretrievable mistake. They
> are led to conceive it is their wisest policy, to shut their eyes
> upon realities, happy, if, by any perversion of intellect, they
> can persuade themselves that they were right in their first
> crude opinion of each other. Thus the institution of mar-
> riage is made a system of fraud . . .

Yeah there's not a lot of room for misinterpretation on how he feels. As a college student I was fascinated to learn that someone publicly criticized the institution of marriage before

the 1970s. A few years after this was published, Godwin met a
woman named Mary Wollstonecraft. She, like he, had radical
thoughts and wasn't afraid to publish them. She wrote one of
the first great feminist manifestos called *A Vindication of the
Rights of Women* (1792). She also had reservations about marriage—her primary concern was how women were treated behind closed doors. Mary had good reason for this. As a teenager
she often slept outside her mother's bedroom to offer whatever
protection she could in the event her father went into one of his
regular rages. She and Godwin were a strangely perfect
match—two souls skeptical of establishment finally meet.

You can imagine the back peddling the two of them had to
do when they decided to get married—Godwin especially.
They married because Mary was pregnant and they wanted
their child* to be considered legitimate. The reason doesn't really matter, however. When you've started sentences off with,
"The evil of marriage . . ." you are going to endure some criticism if you marry, but marry he did. No one stopped him. I
doubt anyone would stop comedian Bill Maher from getting
married either. He once told *Rolling Stone*, "I always compare
marriage to communism, they're both intuitions that don't conform to human nature, so you're going to end up with lying
and hypocrisy." Were Maher to announce an engagement, he
would have to deal with a rhetorical flogging from the late-
night circuit. After that, I'm sure his fellow comedians would
congratulate him and send a gift.

---

* This is neither here nor there, but if it ever comes up in a game of
  Trivial Pursuit: Their daughter, Mary Godwin, later Mary Shelley, is
  the author of *Frankenstein*.

If you're on the fence about marriage, public opinion will sway you toward favoring it. If you have your cynical skin on, however, public opinion loses much of its power and you'll view marriage more pragmatically and less fancifully. Those who have made special arrangements to be called a hypocrite in order to wed, such as Godwin and Maher, will likely be extra certain that they want to go through with it. This is why I see no harm in looking at any establishment with a suspicious eye—even out loud. It makes for more informed decisions. You can say you examined a situation from many sides before making a determination. If you are openly cynical like Godwin and you meet someone worth being a hypocrite for then so be it. Sometimes eating your words is well worth it.

On September 3, 2000, at the age of sixty-six, feminist icon Gloria Steinem did the matrimonial back pedal. She spent thirty years prior to that saying things like, "The surest way to be alone is to get married." She worked tirelessly to make marriage the significantly more equal institution that it is today. Still, she had no intention of taking advantage of marriage herself. Then one day she fell in love. She fell in love with David Bale—actor Christian Bale's father. After they married Gloria released a statement saying, "I'm happy, surprised and one day will write about it, but for now, I hope this proves what feminists have always said—that feminism is about the ability to choose what's right at each time of our lives."

I encourage you to take a walk on the cynical side. Stop watching engagement videos on YouTube. Instead, read an infidelity memoir or two. Play celebrity divorce watch. It won't take away your desire to love—scout's honor. I met Frank after I became a semi-skeptic, and I was still transported right back to seventh grade in his presence. There was, however, some balance between the two opposing forces. Cynicism takes the edge off infatuation, or maybe infatuation waters down cynicism. My hope is that, in a lasting relationship, the mixing of these two perspectives ends up equaling something that is both whimsical and practical. Spontaneous and concrete. Excited yet informed. If anything can soften a cynic it will be love. And a heaping spoonful of cynicism might just bring those starry-eyed expectations back down to earth. It's official: I am center-leaning cynical.

MIDLIFE TRIUMPH

I was standing on the corner of 72nd and Broadway talking to my mother when she gave me a startling family update: "Your Aunt Wynn and Uncle Mortimer are getting divorced." This was very strange news. I was twenty-seven at the time and Wynn and Morty had been married longer than I had been alive—about thirty-five years. I asked what happened, but my mother had limited details.

Growing up, my cousins and I considered a trip to Wynn and Morty's the greatest adventure. Their homes were enormous—at least five bathrooms to play in—and always included some fabulous feature like a ballet studio, hot tub, sauna, or other enhancement that didn't exist in the suburbia from whence we came. Wynn is the oldest of seven children and, having had her fill of screaming babies, decided early on that a career would be her priority. While living in Manhattan she met Morty—an equally career-driven coworker who also had no plans to have children. She was twenty-seven when they married at the UN Chapel and, as she says, "I got married way younger than I had planned to." Oh how I admire that it was the 1970s and her plan was to marry *way* later than twenty-seven. Alas, love came along and there was no reason to delay.

Wynn and Morty worked hard, traveled often, and every few years moved from one extraordinary house to another. All my life they had lived on the east coast, but when I was a sophomore in college they headed west to California. After several years of living there, the decision was made to separate. My initial question about what happened was answered in due time. Morty remarried shortly after the divorce.

Since I'm telling this from my perspective, I can't speak directly to the hurt it caused Wynn. I want to acknowledge the emotional disruption without assuming I know exactly what her toils were. What I saw from the outside, however, was nothing short of amazing. She took back her maiden name and returned to the east coast to live closer to her family. There, she purchased a lovely home where she hosts many of our family gatherings. My cousins and I whispered to each other, "So, um, do you see how well this is being handled? Me too. Okay cool. Just checking." We were fascinated by her when we were little and we continue to be.

After a year of settling in, Wynn had an announcement—a child might be in the cards for her after all; she had decided to adopt. She began the process and met a spirited fourteen-year-old named Cynthia. It was love at first sight. As you can imagine, Cynthia had had her heart broken a few times as well. Now they live, learn, love, and heal together. On adoption day Wynn told the judge, "I never knew I could love someone so much." I relayed this story to a friend and he asked if I thought

her adopting meant she'd always wanted to have children. I
don't think so. Rather, I think the wind changed in her life,
and she adjusted her sails like nobody's business. My family
adjusted its sails, too—following her lead. Wynn didn't vilify
Morty, so we didn't vilify him either. Although the first year
there were a few jokes made in his honor around the Thanksgiving table—and rightly so. We now say "Wynn and Cynthia" the way we used to say "Wynn and Morty," as if it's been
this way all along. And that is my Aunt Wynn's recipe for lem-
onade.

*God breaks the heart again and again and again until it stays
open.*

—Hazrat Inayat Khan

TEN

HOW DO I LOVE ME?
LET ME COUNT THE WAYS!

When you thought you'd be baking pie & living behind your very own white picket fence, you'll find yourself doing something so entirely different, you couldn't have even imagined it a year before. There will be moments when you'll look around and not even recognize your own life ... in a good way.

—Kate Northrup

I've been hard on Walter Elias "Walt" Disney (1901–1966)—tearing his classic stories to shreds. But I relish those tales. I can name all the princesses, and I could probably recite *Sleeping Beauty* by heart if I had to. He was an influential and talented man. No individual has been nominated for more Academy Awards (fifty-nine) and no one has taken more home (twenty-two) than Mr. Disney. He created one of the (if not *the*) most recognizable brand(s) the planet Earth has seen, and he wanted to make people happy with his work. It's a noble aspiration and I commend him. We just disagree on how it's done.

Walt asserts that happiness exists over there—in that castle and with that person. I, on the other hand—under the influence of my boys Erich, Eckhart, and Don—have come to believe that living in the present and working through whatever circumstance the moment has to offer is the way to consistent and genuine joy.

Disney fairytales posit that there is one dragon to slay, someone else will slay it for you, and on the other side of that afternoon kill is nirvana—where the skies are not cloudy all day. In reality, however—in life, in love, and in friendship—there are many dragons to slay and many villains to face, some over and over and over. And the only person who can pull the sword from the stone and make the monster beg for mercy is you. Pull the sword out, fight the bad guy, and then have drinks with the prince when it's over. *You* are the chosen one. It's you who has to rescue the damsel in distress.

Here are a few guidelines I've found helpful in rescuing myself on a daily basis: Stop trying to live a life that doesn't hurt or one that is rejection free. Embrace your emotions—all of them. Listen to what they are telling you about yourself. If the bad ones linger too long, ask them why they've come to visit. Either in a meditative state, in your journal, or some other imaginative way, ask disappointment, sorrow, and anxiety why they keep coming around. The answer won't come immediately. Be brave enough to ask and open to receiving the response. Remember that you are the common denominator in all of your problems. This is not bad news—it means you are also the solution. Transformation will come when you stop blaming other people or circumstances for your anguish. Take responsibility for the role you play in your troubles. Change that which is in your power to change and accept when a state of affairs is beyond your control.

Now is a good time to turn off autopilot. Stop doing things just because you've always done them. Ask yourself—to the point of being annoying—what the purpose of everything you're doing is. Why stay in this friendship even though you find yourself ridiculed regularly? Why make the man's bed and do his dishes when he doesn't know your last name? Why habitually apologize to everyone for things you didn't do wrong? When the layers are peeled back, you will often find that the pit of the fruit is made of fear. "I'm afraid . . . to admit that he doesn't feel the same . . . to say good-bye to someone I've known my whole life . . . that even though he doesn't treat me very well, he's my only chance for love." Once you've identified the specific fear that's paralyzing you, you've got your first dragon to slay. If things do work out with the aforementioned prince, there will be villains to take down together, and it will strengthen your bond. On uncertain days, however, remember that he cannot take down your villains for you and—tattoo this on your wrist—you *cannot* do it for him.

Don't be afraid to ask for help. Whether you feel drawn to professional aid, a spiritual guide, a twelve-step program, or books—seek mindful mentors. People have been where you are. Some were there yesterday, others two hundred years ago. Be open to their teachings. The one thing you cannot do is nothing. You cannot do exactly what you've been doing all along and expect new results. Give up humdrum habits and replace them with purposeful practices. Be bold. Take risks. Leave room to make mistakes. Love your spirit and the beautiful body it inhabits. Live the examined life.

The privilege of a lifetime is being who you are.

—Joseph Campbell

FIND THE ONE IN EVERY ONE

I spoke at the beginning of the book about practicing love. It is possible—I'll argue necessary—to practice love whether you're seeing someone, not seeing someone, or just getting over someone—especially when getting over someone. How do you practice? Who do you practice on? Everyone. This doesn't mean practicing romance on everyone, but romance isn't the crux of love, anyway. It's the other components—patience, compassion, forgiveness, honesty, authentic apologies, and learning to accept an apology with grace rather than with an "I told you so!"—that can be practiced on everyone. If you master these practices with your mother, friends, annoying coworker, and even yourself—then it will be considerably easier to extend the same benefits to your significant other. Oftentimes our expectations of a spouse or partner are insurmountably high, and it can be more difficult to give that person the benefit of the doubt than just about anyone else.

Having to make an effort with our partner contradicts everything we've heard about love, which is that when the right person walks in, it will be smooth sailing from that moment on. When the One arrives, our thinking goes, we will know how to love him; no lessons needed. Erich Fromm is going to give a thumbs down on that notion; he says, "This attitude can be compared to that of the man who wants to paint but who, instead of learning the art, claims that he just has to wait for the right object—and that he will paint beautifully when he finds it." Fromm also professes that the only difference between the love shared with a significant other and everyone else is that you have a physical relationship with your significant other. Everything besides the erotic—empathy, truth, and kindness—is to be shared freely.

Eckhart Tolle sums this truth up beautifully: "Love is not selective, just as the light of the sun is not selective. It does not make one person special. It is not exclusive. Exclusivity is not the love of God but the 'love' of ego. However, the intensity with which true love is felt can vary. There may be one person who reflects your love back to you more clearly and more intensely than others, and if that person feels the same toward you, it can be said that you are in a love relationship with him or her. The bond that connects you with that person is the same bond that connects you with the person sitting next to you on a bus, or with a bird, a tree, a flower. Only the degree of intensity with which it is felt differs."

What a magnificent sentiment—instead of looking around for another person to justify your entire existence, try sharing love with everyone. One day you'll notice someone reflecting your own love back to you more noticeably than the others. If things don't work out, it simply means he didn't reflect your love, or he stopped reflecting your love. Keep sharing love until you spot another intense reflector. When we give to another, that's love. When we take, that's ego. In my most desperate moments of wanting a certain man to be with me I would have shouted, "But I just want to love him!" The truth, however, is that I wanted *him* to love *me*—to save me, to give me purpose.

If my focus is on my desire to love someone and he doesn't respond, I will recognize and respect that he doesn't feel the same.* In contrast, if I focus on wanting someone to love *me*, all evidence to the contrary, I won't stop getting in touch. My ego won't get the memo.

YOU ARE NOT ALONE IN BEING ALONE

Change is here. We don't have to wait. In my life so far, there have been significant societal shifts. Gay marriage wasn't part of the conversation in 1979, but it is now part of a global conversation and legal in a number of states and almost half of the countries in Europe. Women officially earn more college degrees than men across the board—associate's, bachelor's, master's, and doctorate. In 2013, a Pew Research study announced that women are the sole or primary breadwinners in 40 percent of homes. Sixty-three percent of these women are single, while the remaining are married mothers bringing home more bacon than their husbands. This is not Ward Cleaver's America anymore, and it hasn't been for a long time. This is a good thing. Let's not forget how hard people fought to break free from the constraints of the 1950s as demonstrated by the Civil Rights Movement and the Women's Liberation Movement. The past wasn't perfect—it only looks that way in photos.

Why then do we continue to believe the non-nuclear family is less than any other family? Because preconceived notions are the last to die. The double standard still has a hold on us even

---

* This is made more difficult to determine when he happily hooks up with you, I know. Remember, ambiguity means no.

though women have made monumental gains in their personal and professional lives, and single people continue to feel like occasional outcasts even though they are quietly taking over the country. In early 2012 Eric Klinenberg, professor of sociology, public policy, and media, culture, and communications at New York University released a book entitled *Going Solo: The Extraordinary Rise and Surprising Appeal of Living Alone*. He states, "In 1950, only 22 percent of American adults were single. Today, more than 50 percent of American adults are single, and 32.7 million—roughly one out of every seven adults—live alone. People who live alone make up 28 percent of all U.S. households, which makes them more common than any other domestic unit, including the nuclear family." Well, look who's the majority now. It's a bad time to be a conformist. Do you abide by the old ideal or the up-and-coming one?

This does not mean there are 32.7 million crazy cat ladies living in the heartland. *Going Solo* explains, "For the first time in human history, great numbers of people—at all ages, in all places, of every political persuasion—have begun settling down as singletons." Some are young and professional. Others are seasoned and making a new life for themselves post-divorce. Others still never married. They are men and women of all sexual orientations. They have careers, community projects, volunteer aspirations, and active social lives. This looks like Mary Tyler Moore's America to me.

The relationship status of these millions of singles is anybody's guess. Single and satisfied. Single and searching. Single and falling head over heels. Single and nursing wounds. Living in separate places but comfortably in love. French philosophers Jean-Paul Sartre and Simone de Beauvoir (both on the never-married list) were in a relationship together for forty-one years. They maintained separate homes the entire time, never living together—though they are buried next to each other. They found a situation that worked for them and went with it—their love being just as profound as any other couple. I'd argue more profound; they were philosophers after all.

Numbers aside, singles know that being single does not necessarily feel trendy—yet. It is, therefore, appreciated when people challenge perspective itself. In 2004, a single, San Francisco–based mover and shaker named Sasha Cagen published her first book: *Quirkyalone: A Manifesto for Uncompromising Romantics*. The concept as it is defined on Quirkyalone.net: "Quirkyalones are people who enjoy being single (but are not opposed to being in a relationship) and prefer being single to dating for the sake of being in a relationship. It's a mindset. It's about being present to possibilities in being deeply single or deeply in partnership. It's also a mindset that recognizes the value of significant others, plural: friends. Quirkyalone is not anti-love. It is pro-love. It is not anti-dating. It is anti-compulsory dating." Yes! What she said. While the word *quirkyalone* doesn't exactly roll off my tongue, the theory resonates deeply with me. I've never had a problem being single between boys I'm crazy about—they don't come along that often—yet part of me has felt guilty about this because it's just not normal. Then one day, someone was brave enough to say being alone in the meantime is okay, too, and I am daring enough to agree.

The concept of quirkyalone might not ring true with you, which is fine. I present it as an option. This is what movements are all about—giving people options. We are part of a mass exodus from the old way to the new way. Our lives are no longer predetermined for us. Whether you have chosen your situation or your situation has chosen you, there are many adventurous options before you. Don't feel bad because your life doesn't look like a very old copy of *Good Housekeeping*. Next time you feel like the only never-married around, know that it couldn't be further from the truth.

SELF-LOVE VS. NARCISSISM

With all this talk of self-love, some might worry about crossing the line into narcissism. We all know people who think highly of themselves in a haughty way. We've dated these dudes and it's not pretty. What we've been doing all along is playing opposites—taking everything we thought we knew and realizing the contrary is true. For example: I want to call the boy / It takes more strength not to call the boy. Jealousy is evidence of love / It's evidence of insecurity. Being alone is bad / Being alone is conducive to love. I'll change him / I cannot change him or anyone. Love is easy / Love is a great challenge. This method can also be applied to the conceited person. He loves himself too much / He is void of such a genuine emotion.

Take it away, Professor Fromm: "The selfish person is interested only in himself, wants everything for himself, feels no pleasure in giving, but only in taking. He seems to care too much for himself, but actually he only makes an unsuccessful attempt to cover up and compensate for his failure to care for his real self." The narcissist needs to believe he's better than others to get through the day, but the person who loves himself looks at all others and sees an equal. Therefore it's fine to think highly of yourself, so long as you think just as highly of others.

Most of us are a mix of narcissistic tendencies and the ability to give generously, and it can be obvious where the insecurities lie. The intellectually insecure person feels the need to assert how smart he is. The self-doubting woman fishes for compliments. Whereas the person brimming with self-love knows what love is. She also knows that love as well as happiness, intelligence, talent, and kindness speak for themselves. You don't have to tout these things to make sure others know you have them; they shine brightly enough on their own. If there's something the self-loving person needs from a partner, she will ask, or have a discussion about what she feels is missing. The selfish person will play games—perhaps try to induce jealousy—and get angry when her partner can't read her mind.

Women can be selfish and demanding, absolutely, but if a person is a narcissist down to the bone he will most likely be— forgive me—a man. In his book *A New Earth*, Eckhart Tolle states matter-of-factly, "Although women have egos, of course, the ego can take root and grow more easily in the male form than in the female. This is because women are less mind-identified than men." It's important for us to be aware of this because it's easy to fall for narcissists. They are charming, irresistible, and say everything our insecurities want to hear. In time, however, chasing after this type, or being in a relationship with him, is emotionally taxing and demeaning. Final thoughts on the narcissist from Fromm: "He can see nothing but himself; he judges everyone and everything from its usefulness to him; he is basically unable to love."

To move away from narcissistic tendencies and closer to self-honor, self-worth, self-awareness, and unmitigated generosity, ask not what love can do for you but what you can do for love. Love defies logic. The more you give to others, the more you have for yourself. It's as contagious as fire. By lighting others' torches you don't extinguish your own. And if you tend to your flame, it can grow into a bonfire—a beach bonfire that welcomes all passersby. Your fire will be where the party's at.

I did then what I knew how to do. Now that I know better, I do better.

—Maya Angelou

I COMPLETE ME

I was walking with Kate one day and she said, "I'm realizing marriage is less this [folds hands together in prayer position] and more this [makes two fists and puts them next to each other]." I enthusiastically concur and appreciate that life has given me a chance to become a whole fist first. When you are whole, you are in a position to look for someone else who is whole—rather than someone you feel the need to fix or who feels the need to fix you. You are also in a position to stay or go depending on what you feel is right for you, because you are a complete and capable person at all times and in all places. It is also possible to gain a strong sense of self when you are with a supportive partner. A woman I once worked with told me when she first got married the idea of being alone terrified her. These days she knows she'd be fine on her own, but she chooses to be with her husband nonetheless.

We unrequiteds have watched our nearest and dearest go through relationships in different ways. Some meet the right person at the right time. When I say the "right" time, I mean the socially acceptable time. The real right time—the authentic time—is whenever it makes sense and comes together for you. For some, the socially acceptable and authentic times coincide, and that's a wonderful thing. Plenty of people meet and marry between the ages of twenty-five and thirty-five and enjoy a long, rewarding life together. In healthy relationships people are welcome to continually discover and develop who they are. Others meet the wrong person at the right time and that comes with different consequences. They may be in for many turbulent years together or they might call it off. Fortunately, the end of a relationship is always an opportunity to discover oneself again.

In my romantic life I've made some bad decisions and had some bad luck. Then again, maybe it's good luck. When all is said and done, maybe it'll be the best luck one girl can have. It's difficult to accept this some days, but the universe is so good to me in so many ways I can hardly believe she's hanging me out to dry on this issue. I'll have to wait and see. I have dodged some bullets—beautiful bullets—but bullets nonetheless. I can say for certain, however, that I wouldn't be a writer without those bullets, so I have nothing to grumble about. While I have no regrets, I do keep a working list of what not to do again. I don't harbor any resentment toward any of the men I've described here—friends or lovers. I am glad I knew them all— even for a split second—and I hope they soon discover, if they haven't already, the gift of being unabashedly honest with themselves. It lends itself nicely to being honest with the women in their lives.

As for you—I hope you've enjoyed our time together, and I hope you feel more comfortable in your own skin than you did on page one. It has been a privilege for me to share these stories and lessons. I wish you a courageous life, full of many—countless—mistakes, each of which is a conduit for learning. May you fail mightily and pick yourself up each time. May you forgive* with abandon—yourself and others. May love come when you least expect it, and may you never lose your sense of self.

May you remember that knowing yourself means the following: 1) knowing when to hold on and when to let go of something or someone—trusting that if it's meant to be, it will be; and 2) being aware that you don't know it all and allowing yourself to be continually taught—by your peers, by those much older, and even by those much younger. May you know that knowing yourself is the greatest thing you will ever do.

I know I said I wasn't going to tie myself to an ending. I changed my mind. (It's mine to change, after all.) I will tie myself to the ending, but I promise to remain completely untethered to the details in between. I invite you to do this with me. How the rest of my life will unfold, I do not know, but I can say with certainty that it will be described in this way. Just before the credits role, white letters on a black background appear: She lived curiously, boldly, unconventionally, generously, hopefully, and, as always, happily ever after.

Thus he is a great and righteous person who, loving himself, loves all others equally.

—Meister Eckhart

---

* Forgiveness doesn't necessarily mean allowing a bad guy to keep coming back but rather wishing him well as you let him go.

STUDY GUIDE

Peope sometimes say to me, "I want to write a book. What
do I do?" If they have a topic in mind, I'll send them a
sample of a book proposal—a thirty- to forty-page outline that
is used to sell the book to editors. Most people grumble upon
seeing it, "Oh man. Do I have to write this?" This is where I
get confused. I'm sorry, did you say you wanted to write a
book?

The same is true of getting to know yourself. People embrace the idea, but putting it into practice doesn't come as easily. You'll know you're making progress when you can point to
differences in everyday life, such as identifying behaviors that
have been removed. For me, this would be: I no longer spend
time with unavailable men; I no longer make my plans around
someone else's schedule; and I no longer visit the Facebook
pages of former lovers.* And then point to practices that have

---

* With the exception of a few with whom I remain friendly.

been added—in my case: I meditate, I journal, I went to therapy for a while, and I continually study.

While there is no one path to the center of yourself, I will leave you with a study guide to help you get started. Erich Fromm said love must be studied, so let's buckle down. I was reading *The Art of Loving* on the train once and a man said to me, "You aren't going to find what you're looking for in a book." I know what he meant. I won't find a relationship with another person in a book. While that's true, I will find understanding in a book and that can lead to greatly improved relationships. The benefit of studying love and all accompanying emotions is finding out what our feelings are really saying rather than what we assume they are saying. For instance, I can't help but think if everyone read a book or even an article or two on jealousy, they would realize that insecurity is at its root. They could then harness that negative energy to figure out what they feel their lives are missing and fill their existence with that very thing. These are some of the books that helped me gain a greater understanding of myself and how I process emotions.

WORKBOOK

Begin with *Calling in "The One": 7 Weeks to Attract the Love of Your Life* by Katherine Woodward Thomas. While I love this book, note that I find the "7 Weeks to Attract the Love of Your Life" promise to be cheesy, and I do not endorse said promise. However if it works out for you, then awesome. Otherwise this book is superb. This is a workbook—a work-on-yourself

book—with one lesson per day for forty-nine days. I encourage
you to take down your dating profile(s) for seven weeks and
concentrate on this. If you're seeing someone you like, keep seeing him. The book will be beneficial either way. While tempting, I urge you not to plow through this book. Dedicate thirty
minutes per day to one lesson. The caterpillar doesn't change
overnight.

REQUIRED READING

While doing the workbook, you can plow through these. I recommend reading them in this order.

> *The Four Agreements: A Practical Guide to Personal Wisdom*
> by Don Miguel Ruiz
> *The Mastery of Love: A Practical Guide to the Art of*
> *Relationship* by Don Miguel Ruiz
> *The Power of Now: A Guide to Spiritual Enlightenment*
> by Eckhart Tolle
> *The Art of Loving* by Erich Fromm

CHOOSE YOUR OWN ADVENTURE

The aforementioned books will help you learn how to be present and to reroute your focus from receiving love to giving it.
To continue getting to know yourself, identify the emotions
and/or behaviors that trouble you and read about them. Or face
your fears—such as the fear of nonconformity—by reading
how others have done it. Sign up to be a student for life. There

is always more to learn. These are some books I've read that
have been helpful in giving me a good old-fashioned change in
perspective.

ON BEING SINGLE AND/OR LIVING ALONE ...

Single: The Art of Being Satisfied, Fulfilled and Independent
    by Judy Ford
Quirkyalone: A Manifesto for Uncompromising Romantics
    by Sasha Cagen
*Going Solo: The Extraordinary Rise and Surprising Appeal of
    Living Alone* by Eric Klinenberg

IF IT TAKES YOU A FRUSTRATINGLY LONG TIME TO GET
OVER SOMEONE DESPITE A STRONG WILLINGNESS ...

Love and Limerence: The Experience of Being in Love
    by Dorothy Tennov
Love and Limerence: Harness the Limbicbrain
    by Lynn Willmott and Evie Bentley
*Is It Love or Is It Addiction: The Book That Changed the
    Way We Think About Romance and Intimacy*
    by Brenda Schaeffer

WE ARE CULTURALLY OBSESSED WITH MARRIAGE.
WHAT IT MEANS AND HOW IT FUNCTIONS HAS CHANGED
MANY TIMES THROUGHOUT HISTORY ...

Marriage, a History: How Love Conquered Marriage
    by Stephanie Coontz

*The Way We Never Were: American Families and
    the Nostalgia Trap* by Stephanie Coontz
Committed: A Skeptic Makes Peace with Marriage
    by Elizabeth Gilbert

TO REALLY PUT A KINK IN THE FAIRY TALE: ROYAL MARRIAGES ARE IN NO WAY SUPERIOR TO CIVILIAN MARRIAGES . . .

*Sex with Kings: 500 Years of Adultery, Power, Rivalry, and
    Revenge* by Eleanor Herman
*Sex with the Queen: 900 Years of Vile Kings, Virile Lovers,
    and Passionate Politics* by Eleanor Herman

SPEAKING OF SEX, EVER WONDER WHY YOUR BODY WANTS ONE THING AND YOUR MIND WANTS ANOTHER?

*Sex at Dawn: How We Mate, Why We Stray, and What It
    Means for Modern Relationships* by Christopher Ryan
    and Cacilda Jetha

ACKNOWLEDGEMENTS

A gargantuan thank you to Dee Dee De Bartlo and Gretchen Crary—for waving their magic wands and bringing this book into the realm of possibility. I am thankful for your invaluable guidance and support. To Kimberly Cowser for her enthusiasm, advice, and of course, for making the divine introduction to Dee Dee and Gretchen. To my insightful editor, Anne Cole. Speaking of chemistry, we have it in spades. It is an endless joy to work with you. Don't ever leave me! To my friend and unofficial copyeditor, Scott. I am infinitely appreciative of your willingness to read my random acts of writing all hours of the day. To my good friend Patrick who is an artist in venture-capitalist clothing. Thank you for your unabashed support of my endeavors and always letting me sleep on your couch. To my sisters: Andrea and Kate. Thank you for bringing me food and water when I had been in the writing zone for too long and for offering encouragement when I needed it most. Sincerest gratitude to my parents for emanating a brand of love so special that I wish I could bottle it and hand it out on the street. I feel like an honorary expert on marriage because of you two. Finally, this book would not have been made possible without my muses: any man who's ever left my heart by the side of the road. Gentlemen, you made me a writer. For this, I am forever grateful.

PERMISSIONS